MARKETING
JUDO

MARKETING JUDO

Building your business using brains not budget

John Barnes and Richard Richardson

An imprint of **Pearson Education**

London • New York • Toronto • Sydney • Tokyo • Singapore • Hong Kong • Cape Town

New Delhi • Madrid • Paris • Amsterdam • Munich • Milan • Stockholm

PEARSON EDUCATION LIMITED

Head Office:
Edinburgh Gate
Harlow CM20 2JE
Tel: +44 (0)1279 623623
Fax: +44 (0)1279 431059

London Office:
128 Long Acre
London WC2E 9AN
Tel: +44 (0)20 7447 2000
Fax: +44 (0)20 7447 2170
Website: www.business-minds.com
        www.yourmomentum.com

First published in Great Britain in 2003

© Pearson Education Limited 2003

The rights of John Barnes and Richard Richardson to be identified as Authors of this Work has been asserted by them in accordance with the Copyright, Designs and Patents Act 1988.

ISBN 0 273 66316 X

British Library Cataloguing in Publication Data
A CIP catalogue record for this book can be obtained from the British Library

10 9 8 7 6 5 4 3 2 1

Designed by Claire Brodmann Book Designs, Lichfield, Staffs
Typeset by Northern Phototypesetting.Co. Ltd., Bolton
Printed and bound in Great Britain by Bell & Bain Ltd, Glasgow

The Publishers' policy is to use paper manufactured from sustainable forests.

Marketing Judo® is a registered trade mark of MarketingJudo Ltd and is used under licence.

To Jigoro Kano who created Judo in 1882. 'Ju' means flexible and 'Do' means way. Judo is about using mental and physical energy rather than just brute force.

Contents

Acknowledgements

'Partnerships' are key to successful Marketing Judo. This book and the principles behind it have been influenced by the many 'partners' we have worked with in different companies, small and large alike, in many countries.

Our time at Harry Ramsden's, now owned by Compass PLC, was particularly important in the development of our Marketing Judo thinking. In that company we had many outstanding business partners, particularly fellow Founder Director Richard Taylor and Managing Director Maurice Gammell. We would also like to thank Graham Parr, Russell Scott, our Non Executive Directors, Franchise Partners, Shareholders, The Bank of Scotland, our advisers Grant Thornton, Mark Copping, John Greenall and all the staff and customers who have helped make it such a great brand.

Our inspiration to keep developing our Marketing Judo thinking continues today from our families, James Horler, CEO of La Tasca Restaurants with his outstanding team, Penta Capital and the other companies where we work, invest and coach.

Preface

This short book is written for people who want to build a brand or business, but don't have big budgets. That's the position we found ourselves in when we bought the one Harry Ramsden's restaurant in 1988. We fell into a way of thinking, which we now call Marketing Judo. In Judo, you lever other people's strengths or assets to your own advantage. In Judo, your mind matters more than your size. In Judo, anyone can become a black belt if they move quickly enough, keep their balance when others don't and train hard enough.

We're not academics. We promise not to use the word 'paradigm' once! This is not another scientific treatise. It's a framework that we have found helpful in developing marketing strategies and plans for companies with small budgets. Above all, it's a collection of real stories and events from which our Marketing Judo moves evolved.

It all started when we gave up our big company jobs, and using the leverage of borrowed money, moved to Yorkshire and bought a fish and chip shop. Twelve years later, having opened in seven countries, floated on the stock market and grown UK brand awareness from 17% to 73%, we sold to one of our 'Judo' partners Granada – now Compass. We have subsequently gone 'back in' applying these moves to our own companies and helping others.

Around the world, big companies have never been so vulnerable. They have been mega-merging, chasing deals and forgetting customers and staff. Small companies can get complacent too. It's always possible to find a competitive advantage, however big your opponent, or small your budget is!

So join us on the 'Tatami' or judo mat. Put on your virtual 'Judogi' garment. Learn how to identify the 'Sloths' and avoid the 'Geesinks', to use your brains rather than budgets, as we take you through our seven Marketing Judo moves.

CHAPTER 1

GETTING THE BASICS RIGHT

基本を正しく

kihon wo tadashiku

Blackpool 1990. The first new Harry Ramsden's fish and chips restaurant to open since 1928, the year Harry opened the original 'hut' in Guiseley, Yorkshire. But there were the doom-merchants:

"It will never work lads. There'll only ever be the one. Besides you're doing it all wrong. No cod, fried in dripping not oil and you've chosen Windy Corner on the Prom. It's Lancashire, not Yorkshire. Bound to fail. You've got the basics wrong."

Friday 19 September. Opening Day. Leverage. Using the power of the media to publicize the opening by getting Neil Kinnock, leader of the Labour Party, to do the Party Conference summary in our restaurant. Using our brains. Costing us nothing. Very clever.

Neil Kinnock agrees because he is playing Judo with us. We have created 50 new jobs and we are selling fish and chips, a true Labour Party food. What better place to be filmed to catch the headlines; to erase the memories of that story three weeks before, when a top Labour spin doctor from Islington had been caught on camera in a fish and chip shop in the North East asking if the mushy peas were guacamole!

The cameras are crowded into the 100-seat restaurant. Neil and Glenys his wife have chatted to every staff member, winning their hearts and minds. Our partners Graham Parr and Jeff Mallinson, friends and families look on delighted. Neil and Glenys sit at the table and wait for the first plate of Harry's Special – 7 oz of haddock, real chips and mushy peas. Mouth-watering. Irresistible sound bites. To be served by a waitress chosen for the cameras, a Barbara Windsor look-a-like.

But we are two weeks late on the opening and haven't had the time to commission the kitchen equipment properly. We are not ready to open and are taking a huge risk. And the Kinnocks wait. And we chat to them about training, about employing the long-term unemployed, and the Kinnocks wait . . . and wait . . . and wait. The cameramen begin to grumble: 'slowest service award 1990?' and the Kinnocks look edgy. We foresee the evening's footage unfolding with headlines like 'No plaice for Kinnock' or 'Has he had his chips?' – a true disaster unveiled to a

NEIL FINDS RIGHT PLAICE!

Source: Lancashire Evening Post

national audience. The frying range had gone down again we realized.

Finally 'Barbara Windsor' appears with the food. The TV cameras roll; the flashes go off; the Kinnocks love the fish and the Judo is working. We have broken one of our rules – Get the Basics Right – but we got away with it.

Then we have to call on another principle of Marketing Judo: 'Keeping Your Balance' (Chapter 7). That same afternoon, John Major the PM announces that Britain is leaving the Exchange Rate Mechanism, pre-empting any media time for Kinnock. We get nothing on national TV or in the papers. After rushing to lever the PR weight of Neil Kinnock, we then had to shut the restaurant for a week to get everything right. Highly embarrassing.

However, we got over our false start and within four weeks there was a queue outside the restaurant and we were turning the tables once an hour 11 times a day. We proved the 'experts' wrong. You *could* sell haddock in Blackpool and they liked the taste of fish fried in dripping. Because it was the way Harry Ramsden had always done it; a basic of the brand. However, we had learned our lesson, the first Marketing Judo move: *Get the Basics Right*.

Don't spend a penny on marketing your business until you know the basics are working.

Go on the Judo mat untrained and you will fall flat on your face. Don't spend a penny on marketing your business until you know the basics are working.

Plotting the course of a new business is a slow, painstaking process. You can't build a brand overnight however much you spin. The cliché is true. The only place you can find success before work is in the dictionary. The dotcom casualties of 1999/2000 proved the point spectacularly. Millions of media dollars were spent trying to rush the creation of so-called new 'brands'. The crowded cemetery of e-failures from e-toys to Boo is undeniable evidence. It takes ages to create brand awareness and get inside people's heads. The new age dotcom companies had picked the Web as their partner (see Chapter 2) to lever themselves forward but they hadn't got the basics right. Their products weren't what people wanted and even if they were, people did not want to pay for them on the Net! Their business plans were flawed.

To be fair to us, despite the Blackpool problems, we were trying to be faithful to the first principle when we took over the one Harry Ramsden's in Guiseley in 1988. We spent all our time on the basics. We started by asking the staff in the restaurant what was working and what wasn't.

One thing they all agreed on – 'T'fish ain't reet!' It wasn't as good as the best local chippie in Yorkshire. You can't spin a yarn to a Yorkshireman on anything, and that goes particularly for their fish. So we found new fish suppliers in Grimsby and went for the best quality we could find. We paid 50% more and never regretted it. Written recipes and standards for every menu item had to be created. Detailed, thorough, back-breaking stuff. It took ages but without manuals you can't get the basics right. We had to invest in new equipment – the first computerized temperature-controlled frying ranges with filtration systems. Service standards. Putting people in the right roles, formalizing recruitment and cleanliness standards.

You couldn't get a pint of beer at Harry's. The pub opposite was living off the queue outside our restaurant. People kept places for each other while they went over the road for a beer. The pub was playing Judo with us! We quickly got our own licence to sell alcohol.

We shut the restaurant for a day and had a training session with a specialist training company. Everyone from the dishwasher to the Chairman learning together on equal terms.

The value of all this was summed up in true style a few years later when we took Harry Ramsden's son to the opening of the Hong Kong restaurant. He turned to the journalist on the *South China Morning Post* and said: 'Lad, if you close your eyes and eat your fish and chips you could be in Guiseley, Yorkshire.' All that hard work on getting the basics right had been worth it!

It takes a long time to become a Dan at Judo. Equally, there are no quick fixes or shortcuts in creating and building a new business or brand in today's fast changing world. If you are in the service industry, there is no point in marketing unless your customer service is right. Service training comes before marketing. If your products are not always in stock at the point of sale, you sort out manufacturing or distribution before you 'spin' into marketing. Obvious stuff, you're thinking? Well, just walk down the high street and see how few get the basics consistently right.

So, if you are starting from scratch, in your quest to build a brand or business, where do you begin? For some reason small companies are suspicious of research. Perhaps it's all those political focus groups that have made us sceptical? Entrepreneurs start with ideas and inventions but too often don't 'ask the customer'. Big companies do the research and then kill the ideas through bureaucracy and a fear of making mistakes. If you've got a good idea and want to build a business, you don't have to hire the professionals to do your initial market research. Use your common sense. Go on a hunt for information. Always take your notebook or palm pilot wherever you go so you can record the facts as they emerge. Hunt through published data – the Web will have it somewhere. Use your eyes and ears. Visit outlets and ask yourself where the weak points are. Read the articles and interviews with leading business people in the market you are investigating. Just about every industry has a magazine devoted to it. It's amazing what people tell you in pursuit of publicizing their egos. Get their annual reports. The numbers in the accounts may be 'well groomed' but the reports on trading and activities will reveal something useful. Get a copy of their internal staff magazines and newsletters. Chat to the salespeople or managers in retail outlets – they know far more about the real strengths and weaknesses of their products than the bosses.

Remember that the biggest companies have the most to lose in today's volatile world, as they can't adapt to change.

But they won't know or admit to their weaknesses. Don't believe us? A very large pub company we know recently hired an outside company to audit their quality standards. Their internal checks by their own staff showed a 90% rating. The outside company using the same checklist and the same marking criteria scored them at 60%.

In the restaurant industry, the staff turnover rate is estimated to be 400% a year, which is an appalling statistic. How can you give good service when the faces change so often? Think of the cost of retraining. Get this right and retain your staff and you'll beat the big boys!

One of the reasons so many companies will not do consumer research is that they don't want to hear the answers. They know they haven't got the basics right. Identify those companies and work out how you can do what they can't. Hunt them out. You want to avoid the really skilled big companies. We call them the 'Geesinks' (see Chapter 3). Anton Geesink is the 6 foot 6 inch, 19 stone giant who revolutionized Judo. You are searching for the ones we call the 'Sloths', they are the ones we like to compete with. Slothful, complacent, fat cats who are ready to be thrown.

Look for large companies who have strayed away from the basics of their origins and entered a new sector where they are struggling. Buying failed acquisitions from them is a great source of new businesses. A large global fast-food company bought a small company in a different sector for £15 million in 1998. Four years and £17 million investment later they sold it to a retail specialist for £2 million.

Another example of an opportunity is in the UK pub sector, where there have been some dramatic changes. Several former 'Sloths' of the beer-brewing world have sold off their pubs. New groups, who have built up portfolios of outlets, have bought these pubs. They lease them to 'tenants', normally small local operators. The new groups then 'securitize' the leases in the financial markets and make a healthy financing margin. However, these financial engineers, who have replaced the old brewers, are increasingly behaving like the old 'Sloths'. They are too big to keep closely in touch with their tenants. They sell off under-performing outlets without really knowing the history. So a new opportunity emerges for the small company who can run a small group of tenanted pubs driven by customer and staff needs rather than the greed of the new Sloths.

Another route is to choose unfashionable market segments, which the Sloths are ignoring. There may be a brand, product or company that used to be big in this sector but has lost its way. Perhaps a Sloth owns one, which the last MD championed. He was fired and it now languishes, starved of care and attention. Perhaps it had a good reputation? This is the fertile territory where venture capitalists plough for management buy-ins and outs. It's what we did when we bought the one Harry Ramsden's.

Everyone in the fish and chip world told us there was no hope for a 'brand'. Fish and chips were apparently about local loyalties to a local shop. Yet our own experience told us that standards see-sawed. People would drive miles to find a 'good chippie'. We asked people why the big restaurant and pub companies hadn't gone into fish and chips. In fact, a few had tried and failed. But they had either tried to copy McDonald's and turned traditional fish and chips into modern fast food or bought little chippies and strangled them with bureaucracy. A big brewer had even tried to turn some of their pubs into fish and chip shops. We realized that authenticity was vital to success in fish and chips, which was why we bought Harry Ramsden's and 60 years of history. There was an obvious gap in the market for a quality, traditional fish and chips brand we were told by the experts afterwards. There always is – afterwards!

Common sense and a healthy scepticism about the conventional wisdom are two key characteristics of a Marketing Judo player! There are lots of businesses out there with history, heritage, myths and anecdotes, waiting for you to buy them and lever them to fame. We call them 'Lost Property'. Hunt them out!

If you have got a business already and want to build a brand, go 'back to basics'. Do some customer research. You are now hunting for feedback. You want to know if you have got the basics right and how you can improve them. Do your customers see you the way you see yourself? Organize a customer evening and talk to them. Put comment cards into your products. We got fantastic feedback from the cards left on the tables in our restaurants. What are the core values of your products and your company? What does your staff think? How often do you ask them? We have an exercise called the Brand Personality exercise. You imagine that your brand is a person. You describe the person in detail. You then build their character into everything you do. You live and breathe the brand personality.

Don't be put off by the vast marketing budgets spent by big company competitors. Mickey Barnes, one of the original copywriters for radio and television adverts in the 1950s (and John's dad) used to compare most marketing efforts to the unsuccessful door-to-door salesman who holds up the product and just smiles at you. Despite the sophistication of today's advertising industry, there is still an abundance of big-budget 'traditional' marketing that smiles at you but doesn't sell; marketing plans that fail to establish clear and simple sales propositions for carefully targeted customers. Wallpaper marketing. Scattergun rather than rifle-shot marketing. And even if they do reach the target, they will probably lose the customer through poor customer service at the point of sale or the nightmare of 'push button' computer voices in their call centres or equivalents. The waste is extraordinary.

You, in contrast, can use the advantages of brainpower and personal contact to beat the big boys. Take inspiration from Stelios Haji-Ioannou of Easyjet who has built a brand in seven years by 'spending most of our waking hours doing our best to ensure that our staff, customers, investors, the media and the public understand *who we are, what we offer and where to find us*'. 'Our Brand', he says, 'is the biggest asset that I own.' His next challenge will be to protect that asset as customer expectations become ever more demanding.

Probably the most important basic to get right is your own mind. You have got to believe that nothing is impossible. Set your sights high. Aim to be a black belt. The vision thing.

We sat in Harry Ramsden's old bedroom in Guiseley and said we wanted to create the world's most famous fish and chip brand. On the back of an envelope! People may have burst out laughing from London to Lancashire, but the people who worked with us went about their work with a different attitude. It was a simple message and everyone got it. We sat the staff down, we sat the suppliers down, we sat the customers down and talked it through. However mundane your job or industry might seem to some, we all prefer to be part of something famous. If you believe in what you and your company are doing, you become more productive. And a few months later, when our backers wanted their money back, we needed to draw on every ounce of that belief. In the big companies there was a saying that if all else failed in your career, you could always run a fish and chip shop. Imagine the ignominy if we had gone bust running one! We almost did. What carried us through was an unshakeable conviction that we were right.

You have to believe passionately in your vision if you are going to convince all those doubters whose money or support you need to back you.

You have to believe passionately in your vision if you are going to convince all those doubters whose money or support you need to back you. This passion stuff is not very

British. But if we could end up selling mushy peas to the Chinese and Yorkshire Tea to the Saudis, then you too can lever your way to your goals. We believe that nothing is impossible.

Try Marketing Judo – but start by getting the basics right.

CHAPTER 2

PICKING THE RIGHT PARTNER

LEVERING THE STRENGTH OF OTHERS

適切なパートナー

tekisetsu na paatonaa

MJ Using the strength of others is a crucial principle of Judo and is the key to Marketing Judo. It will save you fortunes if you get this right. It starts with your own team.

Partnering the right people

It is unlikely you will succeed in building a brand on your own. The obsession in the media and business textbooks is normally with the individual. In the real world, you need a soul-mate, someone who complements you. People choose the most unlikely business partners and get it wrong so often. You need a partner or partners whose strengths you can lever.

If you have worked together before, so much the better since you will understand each other's strengths and weaknesses. The longer you spend on picking your team partners the more likely you are to survive. It may be unfashionable to say so, but you should like your partners! So many British people put on a cloak when they go to work and adopt a different personality. You want to partner the real one, not the cloak. When the unexpected happens (see Chapter 7) you will have to pull on the strength of your relationship to keep your balance.

Belbin developed a simple team-profiling methodology, which is easy to get hold of. Myers-Briggs is another useful tool. Both really help to get under the 'cloaks'. If you and your partner are both poor 'completer-finishers' on the Belbin scale, you need to find someone who isn't. One of us (the poor completer-finisher) has the following profile 'likes to walk on a tightrope but always drags a safety net beneath him'. It's much easier to work with people whose flaws are openly admitted. Picking the right partners is fundamental to creating a climate where creativity thrives and brains are used before budgets. If you are preoccupied with personality clashes, you will stifle ideas. That is what happens in so many large organizations.

In Judo, you train and learn with partners before you compete. You can't play Judo on your own. Building a business is rarely one person's creation: ideas are formed from lots of different people's inputs. Two minds are better than one; you have to pick the right one to partner.

In Judo, you use your partner's strength to your advantage. You look for all the points of leverage.

Partnering the right advisors and investors

When it comes to picking advisors, your accountant, your lawyer, your fund providers, picking the right people to partner makes a huge difference. Picking advisors who are prepared to play Judo with you by working on success-only contingency arrangements is good leverage. You are looking for advisors who have been through it before and with whom you can identify. Pick the venture capitalist investor who has invested his own money in their fund. Find a Band of Angels. The tax climate for high net worth individuals (Angel investors) to invest in you has never been better. The UK is a virtual tax haven for the entrepreneur with currently only 10% capital gains tax after two years on business assets.

The Enterprise Investment Scheme provides income tax relief and a shelter for capital gains. Choose an accountant who can guide you through this and make sure your interests are looked after as well as the lead investors. You need a legal firm where you get a partner working directly with you. Select a bank where the manager has decision-making autonomy, or at least only one credit committee to refer to. Find out early on from your bank how they view your chosen industrial sector: is it on red, green or amber status? How long have the lights been flashing that colour? Who are they backing like you? Find a way to talk to the comparable client or investee company who can tell you the real story. Watch the advisor's fees. If you can't get a contingency deal, get a fixed budget. Fees can be astronomic. A new concept is being developed for bigger deals called a 'deal room'. This is an on-line facility where the forests of legal documents are standardized and costs are fixed.

Can you attract a non-executive director to add size and status to your company? That's great Judo. You want a non-executive who is a coach and mentor. You want to avoid the 'in my days we did it like this' type.

Partnering the right site

One of the crucial partners to pick in retail is the site and location. If you are a new brand and pick a site next to a successful market leader, you are using their strength to get recognition.

One of the long-term successes in UK restaurants is Pizza Express. They have stopped printing all their site addresses on the back of the menu because competitors used them as a cheap way to identify good locations for their new sites.

In 1988 Harry Ramsden's was not a famous name outside Yorkshire. Less than one in five people knew the name nationally. So for our new sites we picked locations next to famous landmarks. We selected the Blackpool Tower, Heathrow Airport, the Hopewell Centre in Hong Kong and the Epcot Center in Disney. Siting next to famous brands and landmarks helped to make Harry's famous. People judge you by the company you keep.

If you need an office location, think Marketing Judo. One of the companies we are involved with has a small serviced office in Berkeley Square, London. The impact of this prestigious address has worked wonders for the company's pulling power in

You can appear bigger than you are by using your brains not budgets.

the USA. You can appear bigger than you are by using your brains not budgets.

Partnering the right franchisor and franchisee

There was no way we could have afforded these sites on our own. We picked franchise and joint venture partners to lever our brand into prime positions and people's minds.

Picking a joint venture or franchise partner can be a brilliant way to accelerate the growth of your brand. McDonald's, KFC and Pizza Hut all became giant international brands from small origins by using other people's money. However, just like choosing your original business partner, you can easily get this wrong. You should never move to this stage unless you know you have got the basics right. Never sell a franchise unless you can show the franchisee that you have a profitable brand and a business format with all the systems working.

We remain fans of franchising as a business concept because it is good Judo. As a franchisee of a major company, you use the strength of their brand and experience to build your own business. The drawback is that you don't own the brand. But if you are clever you learn enough to go on and lever all this experience to create your own brand next time around. We have watched countless franchisees do this internationally.

Equally, the big brand-owning franchisor/Goliath can play Judo with the small entrepreneurial local businessman. He can 'act small' in a way that the Goliath never could. The local franchisee knows his community well. He can give the brand a local accent that the customer recognizes. For that reason, we particularly favour franchising if you want to set up an international business. Franchisees can bring entrepreneurial thinking and ideas to otherwise Sloth-like companies.

Partnering the right celebrity!

Picking a celebrity as a partner to publicize your business has obvious appeal. An old cliché in marketing says if you run out of ideas, use a celebrity. Celebrities cost a lot. Soccer players are now negotiating their playing contracts on the basis of their 'image rights' as well as their value as players. They see themselves as brands. Celebrities are risky – they sometimes get arrested for unmentionable offences. Celebrities are not a substitute for getting the basics of your business right.

The original Harry Ramsden was a master of the art. He used to get famous sports stars, politicians and performers to eat in his restaurant – and pay for their meals! Wilfred Pickles, Gilbert Harding from radio, Brian Close – an endless list. Show business also ran in the family: Harry's nephew was Harry Corbett, the creator of Sooty. He used to play the piano in the restaurant with the famous glove puppet on his hand! It became a place to see famous people in Yorkshire.

Learning from Harry, we invited Jack Charlton, the footballer, to speak at one of our shareholder evenings in the restaurant. We told him of our plans to open in Dublin where he was a national hero after leading the football team to the World Cup. Jack offered to invest in the venture and opened Harry Ramsden's on the Naas Road in a blaze of free publicity. Crowds flooded to the restaurant calling it 'Jack's Place'. Great Judo!

We were delighted when Nick Faldo, as the previous US Masters winner, exercised his right to choose the menu at the dinner on the eve of the tournament. He chose fish and chips. We surmounted the logistical difficulties and provided the real Harry Ramsden's product. The PR was fantastic – and free!

In contrast, Planet Hollywood set up a worldwide chain based on movie stars' fame. Arnold Schwarzenegger and Bruce Willis invested and it crashed into Chapter 11 bankruptcy twice! The first Chapter 22 in the industry! The menu was ordinary and the stars rarely ate in the restaurants. The basics were not strong enough to support the spin.

Celebrities and catering mix well on television, but rarely on the high street. Celebrity chefs have become the darlings of the digital TV channels. Believing their own hype, they open chains of restaurants under their famous names and rent their names out to all and sundry. But they can't get the basics right in every kitchen because they can't be there all the time. The customer wants to see the celebrity or know they have been in the restaurant. The prima donna mentality is hard to 'chain'.

Too many egos spoil the broth. More often though, it usually ends in tears. One celebrity chef was recently reported to have poured vitriol on another by saying that his four-year-old's school canteen served up better food!

Arsenal Football Club played clever Marketing Judo with Japan when they recruited the top Japanese player Junichi Inamoto (now goalscoring with Fulham). They attracted enormous interest for the Arsenal brand in the Far East, even though he never played in the Premier League for them. Manchester United FC have jumped onto the Far East Marketing Judo mat by opening a chain of 'REDS' restaurants over there. This is a much riskier move in our view, as getting the basics right in the restaurant business is so hard.

Cartoon characters are a safer bet for celebrity endorsement. Our favourite is the partnership between Domino's Pizza and The Simpsons. Dough and D'oh! A brilliant combination of cleverly positioned brands. Domino's have succeeded in opening 200 stores in the ferociously competitive pizza sector of the fast-food market by targeting home delivery rather than high street outlets. They innovate in menu ideas (like tandoori topping) and lever the ingenuity of their local franchisee to out-market the local pizza parlours and avoid the big pizza chains. They 'zig' when others 'zag' as we describe in Chapter 6. The pull of The Simpsons to attract kids led to an extraordinary 27% increase in like-for-like sales in one year, which is unheard of in the industry.

The Simpsons also used Marketing Judo to achieve fame. They started life as a short insert in *The Tracey Ullman Show* in 1987 in the USA. Their success led to a unique prime-time slot for an animation programme. The audience ratings zoomed into orbit. Today 60 million watch the show in the USA and it is syndicated to 90 countries. Fox television has reportedly made $1 billion in earnings from the TV show and $2 billion of merchandise has been sold too.

There is even a university course in Simpson Studies in Michigan! All this was created by one man, Matt Groening, who used the strength of *The Tracey Ullman Show* to create a worldwide brand. But again, beware of celebrity endorsements. Even cartoon celebrities can get into trouble. The Brazilian Government complained after Homer Simpson was shown being abducted by a drug-peddling taxi driver on arrival at Rio Airport as Bart sat watching hardcore porno in his hotel room.

Partnering the right country

Building a brand is about adding psychological value to superior products, concepts or services. At Harry's we picked Great Britain as our partner. We made a strong connection to British tradition in everything we did. We used the power and fame of our country against the imported American hamburger chains from the USA.

Learning from this, in our latest restaurant investment – La Tasca – which serves tapas on a grand scale, we are now playing Judo with Spain. No one else is doing this. Customers love the authenticity of being served by Spanish staff in authentic surroundings eating genuine Spanish food. Sun, sangria and no 'Slothing' is our strategy. We are linking with everything Spanish from language lessons to flamenco dancing. People who go to La Tasca have a picture of good times in Spain in their minds.

Caffè Nero is outwitting the other coffee chains by partnering Italy, the true home of great espressos, cappuccinos and lattes. 'The best coffee this side of Milan' is the proposition, with Italian food, staff and coffee to remind you of Italy.

The Yo! Sushi restaurant chain is a master at Marketing Judo, as you would expect from a company that sells food from the home of judo – Japan. Their service system is unique. You pick the dishes from a moving conveyor belt, just as you would in Japan.

Taylor's Tea has partnered a county within a country – Yorkshire – to market the best-selling Yorkshire Tea range. Regions and counties can often provide low-cost, talented Judo partners. Yorkshire has helped companies to build brands in beer, as well as fish and chips and tea. Cornwall has inspired companies to succeed in ice cream and pasties. Levering the power, strength and psychological imagery of cities, regions and countries can save fortunes in marketing.

Partnering the right company

Judo is all about using your opponent's strength rather than just opposing it. This is a concept that doesn't come naturally to most of us. In the corporate world it is more normal to attack than co-operate, to resist the pull of the competitor, rather than going with it and using the momentum to your advantage. Following this principle resulted in 'black belt' success for us at Harry Ramsden's.

In 1994, Richard got a call from Garry Biggs, then Marketing Director of Young's seafood products. At that time, Young's was part of the huge United Biscuits empire. Young's had a range of frozen, battered fish called 'Chip Shop' for home cooking. They wanted a real point of differentiation from the Birds Eye equivalent product. We were asked if they could use Harry's famous secret batter recipe and launch a new premium product to add to their range. Our initial reaction was to be stubborn and resist. We thought of the threat to the restaurant business and our reputation.

After all, nobody else in the restaurant business was doing this at that time. It could 'cannibalize' our fast-growing sales line. Imagine the fiasco if the factory made poor quality product. This would feed back on the restaurants and knock our hard-won quality image. Then we started to play Judo. Unconsciously at first, and then deliberately, we 'went with the pull' and co-operated. Let's get the basics right, we said. We visited their factory and R&D facility in Grimsby to see if we were 'picking the right partner'.

We found like-minded people in Wynne Griffiths and Garry Biggs who believed in the same things. We agreed to develop a batter mix that would beat Birds Eye's product in consumer research by a 'clear blue water' margin. Then and only then would we give the Harry Ramsden's seal of approval. We insisted that they could feature an endorsement from Harry Ramsden's on the packet but that it would not be branded purely as Harry Ramsden's. It took nine months of hard work to come up with a batter that could pass test production trials and another nine months to translate that into real-line production.

The wait was worth it: 18 months later, Birds Eye had been beaten significantly in blind testing. The product was launched in 2500 stores and backed with a massive television ad campaign funded by Young's. It shot into a big lead in market share and even won an award as best new product launch from *The Grocer* magazine.

A range of proper thick-cut chips followed, developed on exactly the same principles, i.e. it must beat the market leader, in research. Mushy peas, pickled onions, brown sauce and tomato ketchup were all added to the line-up. The Harry Ramsden's name was everywhere and brand awareness jumped.

Restaurant sales grew. Young's made healthy profits and we got royalties on every sale, which didn't cost us a penny. By adding the strength of the Harry Ramsden's name to the research and development and marketing skills of Young's we doubled our momentum and threw the competition. Perfect Marketing Judo. By taking on the giants of Unilever, owners of Birds Eye, and McCain's, the global chip company, and by partnering Young's, little Harry Ramsden's succeeded. I remember the first time I toured the tables at

Leverage. Picking the right partner. Going with the pull and not resisting. It works.

The Harry's in the Dome Greenwich, our only outlet in London. 'We love Harry's,' I was told. 'Which outlet have you visited?', I asked. 'None' was the usual reply, 'but we know it's the best because we love the fish and chips they sell in supermarkets!' Leverage. Picking the right partner. Going with the pull and not resisting. It works.

Big companies are getting used to co-operation. 'Two minds and two brands are better than one' is becoming the mantra. Marketing Judo takes this to another level by applying a consistently integrated game plan. By using the strengths of a partner you can save fortunes that would otherwise be needed to get to your target customer. For example, The Carphone Warehouse linked with *Cosmopolitan* magazine to access a large female audience by launching a text message horoscope service sold in their stores.

Companies wishing to improve their 'ethical' appeal are looking to partner charities. The Judo works for both partners – the charity raises funds and the company gets its logo and message into places that money alone won't reach. Microsoft's partnership with the NSPCC for the Full Stop child abuse campaign is a recent example. Another is in the purchasing area, where Judo principles again work. Industry-wide purchasing exchanges have sprung up in the USA using the power of the Internet to combine purchase orders from competing companies and win economies of scale for all parties. Big companies are sometimes willing to 'third-party' purchase for other smaller companies. They both get a better deal. The big company gets a price break by adding the smaller company's volumes on to its own. It keeps a portion of the gain and passes on a lower price to the smaller one. Great Judo. You can spend the savings on marketing!

Partnering the right brand

With Young's, we were levering their research, development, manufacturing and distribution strengths to get our brand into distribution outside its narrow restaurant base. They in turn were levering our brand's reputation. The manager responsible for the Harry Ramsden's and Young's partnership went on to use the same approach at United Biscuits cake division. Cakes made with Milky Way and Galaxy chocolate soon followed. United Biscuits had already learned the value of Marketing Judo by using the actress Jane Asher to endorse a cake range and Linda McCartney to back a vegetarian range of ready-to-cook dishes.

Linking your product, concept or brand to a more famous brand can be a fast and lower-cost way to build your own revenues and reputation.

Companies in the computer games industry often get established by developing games based on the attraction of a well-known brand, film, TV show or celebrity. With the profits from these licensed games, these companies go on to create and publish their own winning titles. They are levering their brand partner's 'intellectual property' to create their own business. Zoo Digital is one such company which is based in Sheffield in the north of England. The company was set up to provide 'solutions' for companies jumping on the bandwagon at the height of the dotcom boom. A timely shift of strategy into the computer games market has led to the ability to partner with famous names like the Pepsi Chart. A deal to publish a top-selling video game featuring Tiger Woods resulted in a great piece of free PR under a big picture of Tiger Woods and the headline 'Zoo Digital captures the Tiger after £1 million coup'.

On the same day, another Yorkshire-based company, Richmond Foods, reported some perfect Marketing Judo moves. Two recent acquisitions, Allied Frozen Foods and the Nestlé ice cream business have made Richmond the UK's biggest ice cream maker. Richmond is focusing on the ice cream and frozen confectionery business, unlike Associated British Foods and Nestlé who have sold them their ice cream divisions. As a result, Richmond has achieved the size and scale to get the basics right and has become the industry's most efficient manufacturer. Now they have announced 'It is all about brands': not their brands but other companies' famous names. They have launched ice cream tub versions of Smarties, Rolo and Fruit Pastilles and Ribena in ice-lolly form. Yorkie and After Eight – two more famous chocolate bar brands – will be launched in ice cream tubs. Richmond are picking famous brand partners and saving millions in marketing costs, which would be needed to establish their own brand names.

In fast food in the USA, different brands are sharing outlets in what they call 'co-branding' exercises. Brands that are more suitable for breakfast, like doughnut or coffee ones, share the cost of expensive prime locations with brands more suited to lunchtimes or the evening. They are playing Marketing Judo with each other. Boots PLC, the UK health and beauty retailer, recently announced that they were abandoning their strategy of opening freestanding retail outlets in South-East Asia. They are switching to smaller outlets located within a local successful retailer called Watson's. They will now be leveraging the reputation of Watson's and their locations to establish the Boot's brand in this very different retail environment, which is a smart way to set up internationally in our view.

Consumers are playing Judo by personally partnering brands to establish their own identity. The businessman who displays the Ralph Lauren Polo horse on his shirt pocket or the BMW logo on his car; the fan wearing the club football shirt; the radio station you listen to; the television programme you chat about – people are partnering brands to establish their status and decode other people's preferences. Picking the right or wrong brand partner can make a big psychological difference. People form intimate relationships with brands; brands are built in the brain.

The big budget bullies think they can buy love for their brands by plastering their logos everywhere. Brains are better than budgets.

Partnering on the Web

In the UK, Amazon are building successfully on their revenue streams from books, music, DVDs and videos by linking up with other famous brands that see the benefit of using their expertise on the Web. The line-up of brands in 'Amazon Alliances' is a Hall of Fame for great Marketing Judo players. The Carphone Warehouse, Expedia, Virgin Wines and Waterstone's have all realized that their brands and businesses will be better off in co-operation with Amazon than in competition. The Amazon brand and the company's profit stream from third-party services are also far stronger when joined with the reputation and appeal of other innovative partners.

Partnering a Judo expert

Entrepreneurs play Marketing Judo unconsciously as they leverage everything that moves in order to survive. We realized we were doing this when we first encountered Compass PLC. This company are Marketing Judo experts. They have built a large global business from a small management buy-out by brilliantly leveraging other people's assets and brands. From airports to railway stations, offices to factory canteens, boats to trains, football grounds to racecourses, Compass is there providing services. The returns on capital employed are so much higher if you don't own the main asset!

In the retail food arena, Compass realized well before other business-to-business contract caterers that they needed to leverage the strength and power of third-party brands to differentiate them. They partnered with Burger King, Pizza Hut and then Harry Ramsden's. Together we persuaded the British Airports Authority to let us open a Harry Ramsden's at Heathrow Airport. Compass provided the fit-out costs, BAA the site and we provided the brand. Three-way tag Marketing Judo. This was the first Harry Ramsden's in the South of England. Using the combined media appeal of the three partners, the opening was featured on the front page of *The Times* business section. The restaurant became a haunt of the stars – Marty Pellow from Wet, Wet, Wet, Boyzone, Rowan Atkinson, Oliver Reed (propping up the bar) and many famous Yorkshire sportsmen ensured high customer and staff retention as word spread of the famous clientele. The awareness of Harry Ramsden's, which had been relatively unknown outside the North, grew by leaps and bounds. Outlets followed in Gatwick, Manchester and Glasgow Airports, all franchised to Compass. Everyone was a winner. We learned how to play consistent Marketing Judo trained by the 'Sensei' experts of Compass. It was fitting that the eventual purchasers of the Harry Ramsden's company, Granada PLC, were acquired by Compass. Your partner who gets to know you well can become your exit route, which all small and medium-sized companies need in this uncertain world.

Picking the Right Partner, the second Marketing Judo move, helped make Harry Ramsden's successful and famous and secured a good exit to a black belt Judo expert.

CHAPTER 3

CHOOSING THE RIGHT OPPONENT

PICKING A FIGHT YOU CAN WIN

好敵手の選択

koutekishu no sentaku

M J Picking the right Marketing Judo partner is all about co-operation and leverage to the mutual benefit of both partners. Win–win. The next move in the Marketing Judo game plan is about choosing the opponent you can throw by using your brains rather than budgets. Win–lose. The right choice of opponent for the Marketing Judo player is the 'Sloth'. The worst decision is to pick on a 'Geesink'.

Spotting a Sloth (*Genus Corporatus*)

Sloth: tailless, toothless, arboreal mammal found in tropical forests of Central and South America. The three-toed sloth has a dense furry coat. Clinging to branches, sloths eat, sleep and travel upside down. They are sluggish.

Corporate Sloths come in many shapes and sizes. The big company animal is easy to spot. He likes to lurk in the head office. The Sloth HQ is a magnificent lair: large glass structures house Sloth-director dining and entertaining rooms, waterfalls, and plasma TV screens. The Sloth's retail outlets in contrast will be starved of money for refits and staff training. The Sloth HQ lair resembles a 5-star hotel where people normally sleep. This in fact, is what staff like to do in the Sloth HQ lair, namely hide and go to sleep in the corporate undergrowth. Their natural habitat is the board or meeting room where captive audiences can doze as the Sloth directors and middle managers drone on in endless meetings A Sloth-boss is rarely seen on the shop floor unless it is to appear in a TV show where he will fall flat on his face. This is because the Sloth is too lazy to leave his safe, comfortable lair and venture into the wild territory beyond.

The Sloth is a fat cat. Sloth directors pay themselves big salaries but rarely invest in the company's shares. They have nosebags full of share options with soft performance targets. A Sloth-boss tells everyone what to do and coaches nobody. The Sloth's business strategy is to buy out the competition and downsize the workforce.

A Sloth-boss never builds up a business or talks to customers. Above all, a Sloth-boss never listens. His team may come up with ideas but he doesn't hear them. His mantra is 'spend, spend, spend' to buy or kill the competition but 'cut, cut cut' when it comes to developing people, experimenting or paying bonuses to anyone other than himself.

Sloth equity is restricted to the Sloth elite. Super Sloth, the number one, has hand-picked the elite on the basis that they will be too slothful to challenge him. Poor Big-Sloth. He doesn't realize that his days are numbered. On the judo mat his sluggish, lazy arrogant approach makes him a soft target. The Marketing Judo predator is waiting to pounce.

Unfortunately, a Sloth lurks in all of us. Fortunately this makes spotting a Sloth company easier, as we can recognise our worst failings in others more easily than we can in ourselves.

A Sloth rests on his laurels – a very dangerous habit.

We opened a stream of enormously successful Harry Ramsden's restaurants. Then got complacent. Our share price was sky high. We did less

A Sloth rests on his laurels- a very dangerous habit.

homework, we worried less and took life for granted. Not surprisingly, the next group of sites were less successful. We remembered that laurels could also become wreaths if you rest on them too long. We recovered our balance just in time.

Small company Sloths abound in the corporate jungle too. They have often started life as another leaner, faster, fitter member of the corporate animal species. Through success, ageing or failing to develop successors they have allowed the curse of Slothery to infect them. They can often be spotted in the undergrowth . . . on a golf course. They dine with fellow small Sloths, recalling previous daring deeds from bygone days rather than talking to their customers or key employees. They have stopped chasing deals or innovating. As control freaks they were good at establishing the business but they are hopeless at coaching others to do things themselves. They cannot manage the next stage of expansion, as it requires sharing and trust, which are traits not to be found easily in the Sloth genes.

Small company Sloths often reside outside the UK in Spanish tax-free lairs, showing a rare burst of speed as they rush through immigration to stop the officials from counting the excessive number of days they have spent in the on-shore UK lair. They are vulnerable. Their days are numbered too: they are easy meat for lean and hungry Marketing Judo man.

Studying the habits of a Sloth company is essential for the Marketing Judo player. The skilled one chooses an opponent whom he knows he can beat. He taunts them, teases them and then tempts them into an untimely attack. The publicity value is huge if you can be bracketed with the big guy when you are really small. Richard Branson's tussles with British Airways attracted big support for Virgin Airlines among customers and the press. Similarly, commercial radio and TV channels have picked out the BBC as a good slothful opponent to challenge. 'Auntie' is very likely to react slowly or bureaucratically to a good challenge.

Some would argue that Marks and Spencer, Aer Lingus and Sainsbury's were metamorphosing into giant Sloths in the 1990s, all the time arrogantly thinking they were still black belt masters. In reality, they were resting on their laurels, living on past successes and failing to realize that size and big budgets were not as important as skill and brainpower. Tesco, in contrast, were experimenting, innovating, listening to staff and customers and building the most successful Internet ordering business in the UK. Ryanair introduced cheap, ticketless flights by using the Internet, while Aer Lingus remained high-price and slow old-economy ticketed. Both were slowly building successful international businesses, without distracting their teams from their core domestic businesses. Tesco have built their international business so well that international operations occupy 66% as much space as UK supermarkets.

On a smaller scale, where most of us work, you can always find a local Sloth. We had the good fortune of being able to target slothful local fish and chip shops as well as slothful chained restaurants owned by big brewers. Many local fish and chip shop owners had made large cash fortunes in their heyday in the 1950s and 1960s. They had failed to keep their standards up as McDonald's changed the customers' expectations of quality, service and cleanliness. 'The fish and chips aren't as good as they used to be' was the comment most often heard in our consumer research. The original owners no longer worked in the shops. The staff weren't well trained and didn't know their customers' names. There remained thousands of really good chippies but now there were thousands of average to poor ones too. By getting our basics right, we were able to take on the local competitor who had got his wrong.

Local car dealerships often exhibit some really slothful habits, worthy of the big Sloths. One of the customers we telephoned to apologize for a poor meal at one of our take-aways told us a harrowing tale about his expensive German car. The dealer had been so attentive when he sold him the vehicle. But when it came to contacting the 'Service' department a few months later, the customer suffered every nightmare of slow, uncooperative, handling possible: the telephone that rang and rang unanswered; the unfriendly response; the headlamp that lit up erratically, but never when it was 'on the ramp'; the failure to return the car clean because the vacuum cleaner had broken. The customer was incandescent about the 'Lack-of-Service' department. How is it, he asked, that I spend £5 on a takeaway with you and get a call from the boss to apologize, but when I spend £35,000 on a car and complain, I get abuse?

It is no surprise that car manufacturers are taking control of dealerships themselves. An exception, like Dixon Motors, shows how profitable it can be to target the local Sloths. Dixon have trained their people obsessively, innovated by partnering with Direct Line in Jamjar to import cheaper cars and set up state-of-the-art supply depots so you can get the car you want instead of waiting for months. By getting the basics right, picking the right partner and avoiding the slothful life, Dixon have sold the company to The Royal Bank of Scotland, owners of Dixon's partner, Direct Line, with big gains for their shareholders.

Spotting a Geesink

Dixon Motors are small company Geesinks. Tesco, Ryanair and the other Dixons, the electrical retailers built by Sir Stanley Kalms, are big company Geesinks. The latter are not good targets to compete with. You have to be sure that you have picked on the 'Sloth' not the 'Geesink'. Yes, the little guy can beat the big one in Judo. However, when the big guy plays Judo too, then watch out! Originally, there were no size restrictions in Judo contests. Anyone could compete. Then, in the early 1960s a 6 ft 6 in Dutch giant called Anton Geesink beat everyone every time. It became clear that size did matter if contestants were equally skilled in the art of Judo; weight classifications had to be introduced. So too in marketing's version of Judo, you must avoid the Geesinks. Unfortunately, there are still lots of them around. Jack Welch, formerly Chairman of General Electric in the USA, led a Geesink company. He succeeded in getting a mega-corporation to act like a small one. Each operating company had all the attributes of the fit, fast and focused player (see Chapter 5).

Geesinks put customers and front-line staff at the top of their value system. Their head offices are positive supporters of the front line and understand their needs because they used to be there themselves. James Horler, the charismatic Chief Executive of the La Tasca business refuses to have a head office:

"Our head offices are our restaurants. Head offices spawn bureaucracy and wasteful meetings and politics . . . Our cars are our offices. We hold our meetings in restaurants so we live and breathe what is happening."

At La Tasca, we want to be Geesinks in each local market we enter. We are not interested in being a big national chain. We are building a big local brand led by our teams in our local restaurants.

Tokyo Olympics 1964: Dutchman Anton Geesink celebrating his victory in the Open Judo category.

Judo was included in the Olympic Games for the first time in Tokyo and the host nation swept up all the Gold Medals except for the Open Judo category in which Geesink defeated Japan's Kaminaga.

Tesco have a head office but their culture is firmly centred on the front line. Terry Leahy, the CEO, holds regular open front-line employee discussion sessions around the business. He clearly listens as they have thrown Sainsbury and seen off all threats, even the rival Geesink Asda!

Geesinks share their success and wealth creation with their staff; Sloths keep it for themselves and their chosen sycophants. Tesco have 100,000 employee shareholders who earned £200 million in bonuses, shares and profit-sharing schemes in 2001. Geesinks set up partnership schemes with their key retail outlet managers, who can earn more than their bosses for superperformance. This concept is hard for old-style Sloth managers to embrace. Geesinks realize that sharing wealth creates more success.

Geesinks realize that sharing wealth creates more success.

How to partner a Geesink

Don't choose a Geesink as an opponent unless you think he is a Sloth in disguise. It is much better Marketing Judo to persuade the Geesink to choose you as a partner for a corporate venture.

Dixons are a giant retailer with a consistent record of growth and innovation. When Ajaz Ahmed, a Dixons shop-floor employee, bought a personal computer in 1995, he asked colleagues how to access the Internet. Nobody knew the answer. His bosses listened to his idea to be the first to get their customers on-line. Freeserve, the UK's most successful Internet Service Provider was created from an employee's idea. Dixons listened to Ahmed, kept 80% of the shares for themselves and allocated the rest to Ahmed and other founder pioneers like Peter Wilkinson, another inspired entrepreneur. Dixons did not try and do it themselves. Freeserve was floated just at the right time to catch the wave of massive stock market valuations in 1999. Two years later the company was sold to Wanadoo, owned by France Telecom for £1.6 billion. The Sloth would never have listened to the idea in the first place. Equally, Ajaz Ahmed would not have been able to get his idea built so quickly without the resources of Dixons.

Small companies can spot trends and quickly produce new product solutions. Big companies with their budgeting cycles and processes take much longer. Even though their teams might react quickly, their administrative systems will not let them move. By backing a smaller company, the Geesink can get the best of both worlds. Rather than be squashed when the big guy eventually gets to market, get him to back you early in the game. Use the strength of the Geesink by a friendly corporate venture.

How to throw the Sloth

If you are choosing a Sloth as your opponent, you can beat him by behaving like a Geesink, even though you don't have his size and stature.

The Sloth spends his marketing budgets on scattergun marketing. The Geesink carries out rifle-shot marketing. He knows who are the highest potential customers, so he can target them more precisely and at far lower cost. He has learned this from loyalty cards and other promotional devices that have given him very detailed information on who is buying his products, when and in what quantities. The Sloth gets his outside marketing agencies and consultants to do his marketing. The Geesink does most of it himself. The Geesink is spending less and less on traditional mass marketing, as he prefers the directly targeted approach.

As we described in Chapter 2, the Geesink uses partnership marketing to stretch his budget rather than funding everything himself.

The Geesink doesn't organize wasteful 'junkets' to launch his products. We were talking to a top car photographer about a recent trip to a high-profile car launch in Italy. The car manufacturer flew the press and photographers at great expense to Rome. The plane arrived at 1 pm. An expensive lunch was followed by a two-hour presentation. At 4 pm, the light was fading. Questions continued. Finally the photographers were presented with the new car to shoot. It was a green car positioned against a backdrop of green trees and green foliage. The new car was invisible. Photography was now virtually impossible. In contrast a rival manufacturer on another launch had no junket and no presentation. They won the hearts and minds and favourable treatment from the camera clickers by giving them a car in the morning, in good light to drive to any location of their choice! The pictures were fantastic and flattered the car more than any words could achieve. Geesinks use brains not budgets. You know which of these car manufacturers you would choose to compete with.

Brains Day not Budget Day

Another company with bigger resources has chosen you as an opponent. What Judo can you play? You realize you are becoming a Sloth. How can you stop yourself from falling asleep?

Here is a technique we have seen used by some successful small companies to leverage the power of their people, companies like Caffè Nero, who have built brands by using brains rather than big marketing budgets. Big companies can use this too.

Those of us who have worked in big companies are too familiar with Budget Day – the dreaded day when you present the plan for your business or brand to the 'grown ups' in the corporate hierarchy. On 'Brains Day' you invite your key front-line employees. You take a flip chart, pens and you become a facilitator. You listen. You stop ordering and telling people what you think they should do. The theme for the day is that there is no budget for marketing. Everyone is challenged to become creative, to develop ideas as you do when you start up a business with little or no money.

You list absolutely every idea, however wacky it may seem. You fill flip chart after flip chart. You prevent yourself from saying how ridiculous many of the ideas seem to you. You listen. Then you ask the team to sort the ideas into a pyramid or hierarchy. They fight for their ideas and then choose the best together. You ask them to rank the ideas on a marks-out-of-ten basis. 'On a scale of 1 to 10 how much do you want to do this?' you ask them. In the final ranking, you and the team commit to do whatever is at the top of the pyramid. You and the team commit together to do everything that scores more than 8 out of 10. If you want to, you can try using The Marketing Judo Game Plan (Chapter 9) as a framework for the day. That's what we do with our companies and in our coaching sessions.

It's amazing what your teams can create. It's more incredible how well it works when everyone has committed to making his or her jointly developed ideas happen.

There is only one part of the Sloth's habits that we would suggest you try. Look again at your business or your competitor's as though you were hanging upside down. Try standing things on their head. Instead of looking at rich Western countries for inspiration, explore the third world's developing markets. Consumers there have tiny budgets, so to succeed, you have to use brains not budgets. A bank in Bangladesh is successfully lending to the poor by pioneering micro-credit. In 1996 this bank lent $1 billion at an average of $15 per loan. Its bad debt rate was only 1%. In India the lack of retail infrastructure and low spending power should make it hard to sell jeans. A company called

Arvind used their brains and distributed pattern kits to local tailors who make the jeans and sell them for $6: they are now the number one seller. Whatever the size of your business or your competitor's, try looking at things upside down. Don't cling to the past and existing structures and cultures; be prepared to change your patterns and habits.

Finally here are some questions to ask yourself if you find yourself dozing off and growing a third toe or a furry skin. Yes, they do seem very basic. But you need to be able to answer them before you choose the right opponent:

→ When did I last have a team meeting when I listened rather than lectured?

→ When did I last talk to customers?

→ How much equity, bonus or incentive pay did my front-line staff get last month?

→ How many of our team's ideas are being implemented now?

→ Did I spend too much time at head office last week?

→ What would happen if we had no head office?

Beware! You are vulnerable. Unless you want to spend the rest of your business life eating, sleeping and hanging like the Sloth, make sure you have chosen the opponent you can throw. The Sloth is your target not the Geesink. Geesinks are there to be partnered not opposed.

CHAPTER 4

GETTING THE CROWD ON YOUR SIDE

THE VALUE OF CREATING YOUR OWN FAN CLUB

味方を増やす

mikata wo fuyasu

MJ Emotional Leverage. Sportsmen through the ages have seen the value of the lift you get from winning the crowd. Word of mouth is the greatest form of advertising ever invented and costs a lot less than TV. Levering the hearts and minds of the crowd to raise your own game. Winning the customers by 'doing the tables'.

It was my second week at Guiseley and I was anxious to show the restaurant team that I knew what I was doing. The restaurant was full. Two hundred sat under the chandeliers, just as they had 57 years before when Harry opened the world's first theme restaurant on the edge of the moors in Guiseley. The new 'Chairman' wandered through the tables chatting away. The staff was watching. They hadn't seen a boss doing this for a long time. No problem for me, having cut my teeth on fried chicken customers in the toughest KFC in Atlanta Georgia. After all, I could win over impatient 6 ft 6 in Lennox Lewis look-a-likes at 1 am in the deep south of the USA with a bucket of crispy chicken and mash! How hard could it be in genteel Guiseley on the plush carpets of the People's Palace, as they called it? Lovely people all delighted with their moist white flaky haddock and perfectly golden chips cut from the best Maris Piper potatoes. This is easy I thought, and how good it is for the staff to see me clearing plates and winning hearts and minds.

Then I came to the table with two sweatered gentlemen. Sweaters patterned with diamond triangles of different colours. I approached their table with a big smile on my face. 'Hello, I'm John Barnes, Chairman of Harry Ramsden's', I parroted in my London estuary tones, 'and how's the fish today?' Silence. Heads down, they continued to eat. 'And how are the chips? – Potatoes are great at the moment', I continued. Silence. Now those familiar with communication styles in Yorkshire would recognize that this silence was not necessarily unusual. Sometimes communication is unspoken and delivered by body language. This is a county where one word is better than two, where 'guff' as they call 'spin' is heresy. So I continued, 'And how are the mushy peas?' Silence. It's amazing in a restaurant how everyone watches. Conversation on the tables nearby dried up. The waitresses nudged each other watching me intently. 'Er . . . and . . . er . . . are you enjoying your meals?' I stumbled on losing my confidence. Silence. By now everyone was watching. I could hear the staff thinking 'How is he going to handle this?' The new Chairman was dying on stage. 'And . . . er . . . is there anything I can do to improve your experience?' I bumbled on, lapsing into corporate mumbo-jumbo. Finally one of the two 'Sweaters' looked up and fixed me with an icy stare. 'Aye lad,' he hissed, 'You can boogger off!'

Winning the crowd isn't easy! But if you succeed you can convert thousands of free ambassadors to your cause. The Marketing Judo is to turn the strength of the Crowd to your advantage. The Romans were great exponents of this art. Juvenal wrote how the emperors would pay people in bread to attend their performances; crowds were 'bought'. Emperor Augustus sponsored Virgil, the poet, to reinforce his connections to the deity by getting himself mentioned

'Aye lad, you can boogger off!'

in Virgil's best-selling work the *Aeneid*. This was the birth-place of patronage or sponsorship, to use today's language. But practitioners of Marketing Judo don't believe in paying for the crowd. We identify more with the gladiators who were slaves; they were allowed to live if the crowd supported them.

The key partner for us to win over the crowd is the media.

The alternative was a gory death if the crowd turned against them. Spartacus is our hero. Like him we have to use brains and skill rather than budgets and weaponry to succeed.

The key partner for us to win over the crowd is the media.

Using the power and weight of the media to gain free publicity is our goal. Richard Branson and Stelios Haji-Ioannou are the Shodans of this principle. Winning over the media and getting millions of pounds of free publicity through outstanding PR have built the Virgin and Easyjet brands. Both companies got the basics right first (see Chapter 1).

At Harry Ramsden's we were inspired by the original Harry Ramsden's showmanship. Shortly after we arrived in 1988, the lawyer of Harry's son contacted us. His dad had named Harry's son Harry Junior. Harry Junior had fallen out with the previous owners. His lawyer told us that Harry Jnr had all these photos and memorabilia. He wanted to help. He looked like, sounded like and acted like his dad. We got on well and eventually provided him with business cards, which read 'Ambassador to British Fish and Chips'. He talked to the Press and told them 'Dad's place is in good hands'. He passed on to us countless numbers of great ideas that his dad had used.

Harry Senior had been a master of crowd-pleasing. On 7 July in 1952 he staged penny-halfpenny day. Fish and chips for one and half old pence. The crowds began to queue two hours before the shop opened. They jammed the streets north to Ilkley, south to Leeds and west to Bradford. Cars filled the car park. The buses couldn't get through. A brass band amused the queue. Harry invited the BBC. Not only did he get radio coverage but also pictures on national television when only a handful of houses had TVs! It was a huge success and the word of mouth from it was still working years later. Wherever we opened a new Harry Ramsden's there would always be someone who had been in the crowd in 1952. Harry understood the power of getting the crowd on your side. Guess who had paid for the 1952 promotion? Naturally, it was his suppliers. Harry would have seen off all competition if someone had staged the Yorkshire Marketing Judo championships.

When we took over Harry's in 1988, it was Diamond Jubilee Year – 60 years after the original shop opened. Richard asked the previous owner's Operations Manager to take him through the celebration plans. 'Well, we've got a mug,' he explained. 'A Diamond Jubilee mug.' Richard asked him what else he was planning. 'That's all', he replied, 'there's no budget you see.' And that was that. This was an insult to Harry's memory: 60 years marked only by a mug! You could feel his ghost shaking his head in disgust. No joke, because we had heard all the stories of sightings of Harry's ghost in his old house where we worked.

It's amazing how many times you can find examples of successful marketing in the past history of a brand. Nothing beats an old success! We re-ran the 1952 promotion with a twist that we thought Harry would have been proud of. We invited the *Guinness Book of Records* to attend the 2p day in October. In partnership with the *Yorkshire Evening Post*, we began a search to find the twins who had been photographed as young girls at the front of the queue in 1952. The newspaper ran Reader Offers and we avoided the cost of advertising. The twins were tracked down and asked to head the queue again. The day repeated exactly the formula of 1952 and got the same amazing results. We sold 10,182 portions of fish and chips in the day. Norris McWhirter of the *Guinness Book of Records* verified the result and it appeared in the following year's edition.

The story was reported in every national newspaper and on national BBC TV news. Massive free advertising worth an estimated £3 million was generated with no budget. The entry as 'the world's largest fish and chip shop' in the *Guinness Book of Records* put us in very good company alongside McDonald's who were the only other entry as the 'world's largest restaurant company'. This appearance beside McDonald's gave us a stature way beyond the size of the company. We had invited all the local community, councillors, suppliers and media and 'worked' the crowd hard all day. The friends we won that day stayed with us for years, many becoming shareholders when we floated on the stock market a year later. The entry in the *Guinness Book of Records* became a superb selling tool when we looked for partners abroad. We went on to repeat the promotion in Glasgow with our entrepreneurial local franchise partners, Derek Statt and Harry Davis, with the same stunning results. A four-hour queue resulted in 11,964 portions sold on 17 May 1992, enormous free PR, many new friends and another entry in the *Guinness Book of Records*.

Levering the strength of the media works wonders for the small company with 'brains but no budget'. Judo teaches you to think before you resist, to move with an opposing force using momentum to your advantage. So many businessmen are uncomfortable with the media and resist journalists rather than co-operating. Journalists have a tough life; meeting deadlines to fill a paper or file a radio story every day is very hard work. Businesses are full of great human life stories waiting to hit the press. People love reading about, hearing or seeing people like themselves in the media. That is why soap operas continue to top the ratings.

Marketing Judo practitioners go with the media and co-operate at every step. There are techniques to be learned and Media Training is a training course that is worth its weight in gold. Small companies attract the sympathy and interest of the crowd. Big companies, particularly global ones, are out of favour. It's the day of the little guy and that is great news for those of us who want to apply Marketing Judo. The big Sloth-like companies dare not speak to the press. They delegate to Corporate Relations departments and PR companies who write boring PR releases that journalists ignore. In contrast, we talk to the media ourselves, create stories based on fact and human interest and never say 'no comment'. Our objective is to become the local media spokesperson for our industry. If there is a story, we want our company's name in it. Even if things go wrong, we are still available to the press to talk about it and explain what happened. Everyone makes mistakes and it's so much better to admit it rather than pretend or spin the truth.

We built on our early success with the *Guinness Book of Records* Day and went on to get enormous coverage. It doesn't work if your basics aren't right (Chapter 1) or if you've picked the wrong partner (Chapter 2), but the upside of co-operating with and helping the media is huge in this media-conscious age. Your staff love reading about their companies and themselves. There are so many heroes and heroines working with you doing charity things, helping others, breaking records, learning new things, and overcoming hurdles. Stories are everywhere waiting for an audience. You can be sure that the Sloth's PR people will be focused on getting the big boss's face in the papers because that's how they keep their jobs! Boring stuff that only interests the other fat cats. In contrast, real-life stories about people whom your customers can identify with will win you hearts, minds and business.

In the Spanish restaurant business, La Tasca, the team scored an early PR goal in Glasgow. Our Deputy Manager at the time, Miguel, was a member of the Real Madrid football supporters' club. The final of the European Champions' Cup was due to be played in Hampden Park, Glasgow, against the German team Bayern Leverkusen. Miguel invited the Real Madrid supporters' club to use the restaurant as their meeting point. Supporters arriving at Glasgow Airport asked everyone for directions to La Tasca. By midday the restaurant had run out of San Miguel beer. By 2 pm there were crowds of two to three thousand blocking the road outside the restaurant. By 5 pm, Miguel was inundated with requests for media interviews about the extraordinary scenes. He was even seen by his mother on Spanish television back home in Madrid. The restaurant had a record sales day and ran out of beer three times.

Getting the crowd on your side means working hard with the local communities where your business is.

Getting the crowd on your side means working hard with the local communities where your business is.

The Geesink Tesco is one of the few British retailers to succeed brilliantly in South-East Asia. 'Harness the wisdom of the anthill' is an old Chinese proverb. Tesco management do it all the time and not just in the UK. In Korea they have partnered local giant Samsung. They now have five of the country's top ten retail outlets in sales terms. Their brand is called 'Homeplus'. They listened to their staff and customers and set up classrooms in their stores for cookery and information technology, and provided nursery and crèche facilities. They discovered by listening that women customers' preoccupation is with education and learning. To satisfy this need they provided classrooms instore. Staff want to work there and customers prefer those stores to competitors' outlets.

Work the crowd. Accept the invitations to talk to local business or community groups. Allow your staff to work for local charities in return for extra paid leave. Your team's motivation will grow in line with your own brand or company's local reputation. Get your business involved with the local college or school. Talking to schools about business as part of the 'business dynamics' programme is very worthwhile. You get an opportunity to 'pitch' your company's credentials and put a human face to your products. The questioning can be more illuminating than many a review with stock market analysts!

Galaxy Radio 105 FM in Yorkshire pioneered a Radio Academy for 16–18-year-old school pupils. Twelve weeks' hands-on training in all aspects of radio from producing and writing to actual live presenting is provided free. Galaxy's success in building the largest listening audience of any commercial radio station outside London has been won by this kind of commitment to the local community. Nobody understands the power of word-of-mouth endorsement better than the radio industry. A London-based presenter with a dance music station took this to a new level. His station's budgets were cut back because of a drop in radio advertising revenues. Using his brains, he developed ways to get his listeners to advertise his show for nothing. This was inspired Marketing Judo. He even asked them to help build his audience, not by word of mouth, but by 'use of hand'! Listeners revelled in finger-ing his show's title in the dirt on cars, lorries and even police cars!

Winning the support of the local politicians and decision-makers is another important source of free brand building. Jeddah, Saudi Arabia, was the venue for Harry Ramsden's first entry to the Middle East. Our prospective franchise partner explained that it was crucial to see the Mayor of Jeddah before proceeding with the venture. On the first day we went to his office and joined a throng of people waiting outside. There was no apparent queuing system. We waited and waited. Two hours elapsed before an official emerged to say that the Mayor had left for the day. We returned the next day and waited three hours before the official re-emerged to say the Mayor had left again. The franchise partner explained that it was vital to keep trying until we saw the Mayor – it would be considered very rude to leave the 'queue'. On our fourth visit and after three hours my patience had just about disappeared. Luckily the official appeared after three hours and we were ushered into the Mayor's chamber with ten others. I was the only Westerner. Presentations began which we all had to listen to. An incredible model of a sculpture for a roundabout was pitched to the Mayor in Arabic. It was probably the most obscure piece of art I have ever seen. Presentations of pictures, plans and books all followed. I had no idea what purpose they served. Nobody left the room. Finally the Mayor turned to me and said 'Your turn'. I handed out a printed chart presentation in English and gave a 15-minute oration about Harry's. Everyone stared at me expressionless, including the Mayor. There was a long silence when I finished.

Three days were apparently about to be wasted. In this case it seemed that Marketing Judo was not working. Then the Mayor spoke: 'I know your company, Mr John.' I was dumbfounded. 'I like haddock and chips.' I was speechless. 'Er . . . How do you know us?' I stuttered. 'I eat in your Blackpool restaurant', he replied. 'You see, I came to Blackpool to buy the Blackpool Illuminations for our seafront at the Jeddah Corniche. We will welcome you warmly to Jeddah.' He became a great help and supporter. The effort to get the crowd on our side had worked from one Golden Mile to another!

Winning the crowd means talking to and listening to your own staff every day of every week and every week of every year. Your people are increasingly your brand. Products are getting harder to differentiate. Everyone in your team should know everything about their company so they can sell it to the crowd with you. So often you hear people working in retail shops complaining about 'Head Office' who do not understand the needs of the real workers. Big companies rarely listen; they lecture their workforce. As an American football coach said: 'Everyone on the team should know the playbook.' If you can get them on your side, you'll win their families, friends, neighbours and countless hundreds they meet.

Studies have shown that every complaining customer tells another 100 people of their bad experience. Equally it follows that a happy employee will tell more than a hundred others about their great company's products. Sounds too obvious? Unfortunately research shows that British workers are the most stressed and demotivated in Europe. This is good news though for those committed to listening to their employees and getting them on their side! There are legions of new recruits out there waiting to contribute to your free word-of-mouth marketing campaign. The mission of Marketing Judo devotees is to serve the people who serve people, rather than stroke the egos of the slothful fat cats.

The highlight of our team meetings at Harry Ramsden's was the annual Quiz Day. Each restaurant sent a team to Leeds United football ground. The quiz was about the business and general knowledge. The teams learned their operations manuals back to front for weeks beforehand. Big prizes were keenly sought after. The title of 'Restaurant of the Year' had some lucrative benefits. On the day of the event, the teams and their supporters came in fancy dress. But there was a special twist: the teams could pick the fancy dress that their bosses had to wear. There was no escape. The Chairman was given the costume and make-up in successive years for such stars as Gary Glitter, Alice Cooper, Pavarotti and, in the final year, Dolly Parton! Everyone learned more about the basics of their business, had lots of fun and stopped the bosses from taking themselves too seriously.

Getting the crowd on your side is the cheapest and best form of advertising ever invented. *Emotional leverage*: that's the fourth move in Marketing Judo.

CHAPTER 5

USING YOUR SIZE TO YOUR ADVANTAGE

HOW TO RUN RINGS AROUND YOUR COMPETITORS

自らの力量を最善に活かす

mizukara no ririryo wo saizen ni ikasu

Being small is no barrier to success in Judo. Vladimir Putin, the President of Russia, has seen the size of the Soviet Union dramatically reduced and the Cold War with the other giant, the USA, come to an end. Putin is a Judo black belt. Studying his handling of the political relationship with the USA, you can see signs of his applying Judo thinking rather than the old Russian Cold War way of saying *Nyet* to everything. He is levering the force and power of the USA to his advantage rather than resisting it.

Just as the former giants of world politics have seen their empires break up, because people want to belong to smaller countries and communities, so in the business world, customers and staff are turning their backs on big brands and big businesses. Hard 'in-your-face' global branding rarely works. The ludicrous fashion to waste budgets on renaming companies with pseudo Greek or Latin corporate names – like Consignia for the Post Office – invites derision from 'the crowd'.

Subtle, local brands and companies are winning the war for hearts and minds. The 'no-brand' bandwagon is growing. 'Viral' marketing is in vogue. This is great news for those of us who are short on budget, but long on ideas.

The small company starts with some real advantages over the corporate giants. Big companies seem to have a manic desire to get bigger, when all the evidence is that people prefer working in smaller groups for the sake of it. Megamergers are happening all the time. A recent study by a big four accounting firm, showed that 92% of corporate mergers failed to show any long-term benefit in shareholder value. This is not surprising if the main logic of acquisition is 'acquire or be acquired'. Where is the added value in that?

There are three advantages we can exploit: to become fit, fast, and focused.

There are three advantages we can exploit: to become fit, fast, and focused.

Keeping fit

Being and keeping fit are key attributes of a skilled Judo player. That means training or *randori* in judo-speak. The small company who wants to play Marketing Judo should set out training programmes for every employee – from dishwasher to Managing Director. Our skills levels have to exceed those of our big company foes. We use brains rather than brawn and have to keep on improving our minds. There are lots of grants available which means playing Judo with the government who want to see small companies prosper. Directors should set the example. So often in big companies, people avoid training by claiming to be too busy. Today's smart employee wants to work for the company who will commit to developing their skills. These are the people who will give most back to you in return.

At Harry's we encouraged our training manager – a former waitress – to do the Institute of Personnel Management diploma one day a week at our cost. She became a key part of our success as we expanded, pioneering innovative programmes like the employment of the long-term unemployed and winning national and regional training awards for the company. These had the extra advantages of getting the crowd on our side (Chapter 4) as we arrived in a new town and created employment. You hear so often how hard it is to recruit 'good people', but how often are the people who say this developing their own internal recruits by investing in their training?

Keeping fit is a literal need for the agile Marketing Judo practitioner. We believe in complementary therapy. We don't mind being called wacky by the fat cats as Yoga, relaxation techniques and calmness under pressure help us stay healthy and create low-cost ideas. Richard and I are based at The Orchard in Leeds where homeopathy, aromatherapy, reflexology and shiatsu massage therapists operate their businesses. We are watching more and more people convert to these new techniques as day-to-day stresses intensify. I will never forget my trips to Harry Ramsden's in Hong Kong when every morning you would see in the parks from 6 am people of all ages doing Tai Chi exercises. The Chinese are brilliant entrepreneurs who understand the importance of keeping fit and the power of mind over matter.

The forward-thinking small company will provide their people with complementary therapy and counselling support services as an employee benefit. The statistics for absenteeism and sickness days are frightening. Helping your team to stay fit will improve productivity, creativity, and give you more firepower for marketing.

Moving fast

The second 'F' word is Fast. Fast movement is a fundamental principle of Judo. Judo instructors teach young children an exercise where they jump around quickly and their partner has to try and catch them to stand on their feet! The faster they learn to move on their feet, the harder it is to catch up with them. Small companies can move so much more quickly than the big Sloths. The airline industry in Europe has seen a sea-change in brand leadership as the fast-moving small companies like Easyjet and Ryanair have outmanoeuvred and thrown the lumbering, over-priced bloated airlines (like Swissair and Sabena) by offering realistic prices and using the Internet and supply chain management to minimize overheads. They are constantly offering new deals at rock-bottom prices and reminding us in the press how much better they are than the big boys like British Airways.

Big companies have slow, cumbersome decision-making processes. There are committees to satisfy, documents to write and rewrite, egos to placate, political agendas to address and, for public companies, analysts to convince. It's so much quicker if you are a small company and keep things simple. It's great fun when you have to negotiate with them. You go to a meeting with maybe one other person. They turn up with 12 and still don't have the authority to make a decision. You move quickly, make decisions and win while the fat cats are sitting in meetings talking to each other, marvelling at each other's debating skills. If you move faster, you are more likely to spot the customer's changing needs. You are more able to keep in touch with your customer while the Sloths are contemplating their corporate navels. You are better able to act before the bigger company wakes up.

Staying focused

The third 'F' word is 'Focused'. In Judo there is one person to throw. You are focused on nothing else. You want your opponent to be thinking about something else; you hope he or she is distracted. At the last Olympics our best British hope admitted his unexpected loss in an early heat was entirely due to his inability to stop thinking about something else! Mega-mergers mean that companies have so many divisions doing different things in different markets that they are unable to focus. These are the opponents we want in the early rounds. All the evidence in the sector that we know best – the restaurant industry – is that the smaller, focused companies are winners. Pizza Express, ASK, La Tasca, Pret A Manger, do one thing well. The failures have been the big brewers who rushed headlong into a growth sector, did pizza alongside French brasseries, American theme bars as well as steak houses, and exited from them all at huge cost with egg on their faces.

We spent 11 years 'doing' fish and chips and nothing else. We were tempted to diversify but, thankfully, stayed faithful to the fryer.

The world is changing too quickly to be able to excel at more than one specialism. The big companies who have succeeded in more than one area are rare. There are some Geesinks – like the Branson Empire and General Electric – that have succeeded by breaking their companies up into small, focused units. They think big but act small. You can throw the unfocused competitor who dabbles in your art. In the small companies where we advise today – from radio to horseracing, from coffee shops to digital game development – we counsel them to 'focus'. In Judo you concentrate on getting another belt. It takes years to become a Dan. It's so hard to get to the top that you enjoy the challenge of getting better and better at one thing. The highest ranking is the red belt and there have only ever been thirteen awarded.

The three 'F' words – Fit, Fast and Focused – are the key to the fifth Marketing Judo move: *Using your size to your advantage.*

CHAPTER 6

DOING THE UNEXPECTED

THE COMPETITIVE ADVANTAGE OF UNPREDICTABILITY

裏をかく

ura wo kaku

Move 6, 'Doing the Unexpected', is about striking first, unbalancing your opponents before they un balance you: the element of surprise! In the cluttered media world with thousands of messages from TV, radio, the press and non-stop advertising, your marketing has got to stand out, particularly if you are short of marketing budgets. Zig when they zag. Your aim is to catch people off balance.

Your aim is to catch people off balance.

When new customers walked through the door of a Harry Ramsden's restaurant for the first time, we invariably heard a 'Wow!' They were expecting a small traditional fish and chip shop and were surprised by the plush dining room with high ceilings, carpets, chandeliers and tables with knives and forks!

When you surprise people, you get their attention. Every week, each head office team member had to telephone at least two customers who had registered a complaint on the comment cards sent directly to us. We had grown from a team of three to twenty-three and were desperate to avoid becoming 'corporate' and fat cats. I telephoned a man who had visited our Bournemouth takeaway section and got cold chips. He had put his mobile telephone number on the card. I introduced myself saying: 'Hello I'm John Barnes, Chairman of Harry Ramsden's and I'm ringing to apologize about your visit to our Bournemouth takeaway.' There was a scuffling sound as he dropped his phone and then he said: 'er . . . er . . . I'm sorry it wasn't that bad, er . . . how kind of you to call. I didn't expect a phone call.' After we had chatted and I apologized I told him I was sending a refund voucher. He became a regular customer, phoned and wrote to me frequently and took a visiting trade mission to eat in the Bournemouth restaurant. It cost us a phone call and a refund of £7. Doing the unexpected.

In markets where product differentiation is harder to achieve, it's the little touch that means so much: the restaurant that surprises you with a bunch of flowers when someone has organized a party for you; the Pret a Manger staff member who ran down the road to give me back a £1 coin I'd dropped down the side of the till. On a bigger scale, Wetherspoon's has consistently done the unexpected by not having music or slot machines in their pubs, and selling beer at very low prices. We gave 'Challenge' certificates to customers who had eaten our jumbo-sized portion of fish with double chips and mushy peas. A former Finance Director of ICI told us he had three certificates proudly displayed on his kitchen wall at home.

Customers do the unexpected too! Judo training tells you to pull when you are pushed and push when you are pulled. That is how you keep your balance. Ken Allen from Harlow, Essex, phoned Larwood House and asked to speak to the boss. When he was put through to me I thought it was a complaint. I was caught off balance. He told me he had visited 15 of the 30 Harry Ramsden's restaurants and had 15 Challenge certificates from eating our 'Challenge' meal. This was a huge combination of jumbo-sized fish, two portions of chips, mushy peas, baked beans, and a free dessert if you ate the entire first course. He had travelled to every outlet by National Express coaches. He wanted to come and see me. My first reaction was to think 'Oh no! This is a mega complaint.' I agreed to see him, a bit reluctantly, and we fixed a date for the following week. He would take the overnight coach arriving in Bradford in the morning. He arrived early and came slowly up the stairs to Harry's old bedroom, which was now my office. I won't reveal Ken's age but he looked very well on all those fish and chips. He showed me his scrapbook of all the Challenge certificates, photos, coach ticket stubs, and told me how wonderfully the staff had treated him. His life's ambition was to eat at every Harry's and get 100 certificates when we had opened that many. I waited for the 'catch'. Surely he was going to ask for sponsorship or payment? I offered to pay for a taxi to take him back to the coach station but he turned it down. He wasn't doing this for money; it had become his hobby. Joan, his wife, thought he was crazy he told me, but he loved it. He was a fan of all things British and fish and chips and Harry Ramsden's in particular – and he came from Essex, not Yorkshire!

We told the press and a deluge of national and local stories followed as he travelled the country. National Express coaches got in on the Judo giving him free travel for life. We even arranged for him to arrive by Concorde at Leeds/ Bradford Airport.

When resources are scarce, necessity is the mother of invention. Doing the unexpected becomes second nature. In 1989, one year after we had bought Harry's, our American Bank had a change of strategy and decided they wanted their money back. We were about to lose our balance. Keep your balance. This is the seventh move we describe in the final chapter. Our private shareholders said they were unwilling to put up any more and no other banks were interested. We were still in the early stages of getting the basics right. We had only one restaurant. A last option other than giving up and selling remained. We decided to do the unexpected. We would attempt a flotation on the stock market, much earlier than we had planned. We had been advised from early on by Grant Thornton, the accountants and auditors who specialize in smaller companies. They introduced us to Greig Middleton, the stockbrokers. There was a relatively new market for small companies called the Third Market, which was the equivalent of the AIM market today. Everyone agreed it would be tough to float the business but they would have a go. Unfortunately it proved hard to get the float underwritten by institutional shareholders, as fish and chips was unsexy and floating one fish and chip shop was unusual to say the least.

We put on our Marketing Judo gear and did the unexpected. We ran a press ad in the *Yorkshire Post* asking people to write in if they were interested in a prospectus if we decided to float. We appealed to the loyalty of our Yorkshire supporters. We were then even more outrageous and persuaded Yorkshire TV to let us put a similar announcement out just before 8.30 pm at a knockdown media cost. We asked people to telephone us. Richard and I together with our wives manned the small telephone switchboard in our tiny office that evening. As soon as the TV ad was over, the switchboard lit up like a Christmas tree. We took hundreds of calls. We got hundreds of enquiries from the press ad too. Very few companies had done this apart from the Gas privatization offer. It had never been done for a restaurant company and certainly not for a fish and chip shop. Doing the unexpected caught people off-guard and they didn't want to miss out. Armed with 3000 names and addresses we returned to the City and the float was underwritten. The Public Offer was two-and-a-half times oversubscribed and we ended up with 4000 small shareholders. They all got shareholder discount cards. That proved to be good Judo as every time the press ran a story on shareholder perks, they referred to the '20% off fish and chips at Harry Ramsden's' benefit. In any event, our shareholders became frequent customers. Hardly any of them sold their shares until we sold the company. Doing the unexpected got the crowd on our side. We kept our balance when we were otherwise heading for a final fall.

We are frequently asked if 'going public' is right for small companies and whether we would do it again. Yes and yes are our replies. We floated too early because we had to; next time, we would want to be bigger. We would also point out that when you are public, you have to move even faster to get growth. Having your growing pains in the full glare of publicity isn't easy, but if you put your head above the parapet, you expect to be shot at! Playing Judo with the stock exchange levered our tiny company into the big league and we got extraordinary press interest. We brought in Nora Batty, the star of *Last of the Summer Wine*

Source: Daily Mirror (Mirrorpix)

(Kathy Staff in real life) to announce the float. Our massive growth in brand awareness was aided by the opportunity twice a year to announce our financial results. I remember after an interim set of results when we had made paltry profits of £80,000 getting full-colour treatment on the front page of the white *Times* business section.

Meanwhile one of the country's top brewers announced earnings of £360 million and was relegated to the bottom of the second page. That morning I got a call from their MD. I was amazed. My adrenaline pumped faster – perhaps they want to buy us, I thought. 'How on earth do you get so much publicity with such small profits, who does your PR?' 'We do', I replied.

Going public was a great Marketing Judo move. It made us look so much bigger than we were. When it came to negotiating a lease with the richest landlord in Hong Kong, he only agreed to consider us because he had read about us in the *Financial Times*.

Nobody expected us to open in Hong Kong: nor did we! Richard got another one of those calls, which you would normally ignore so you can get on with your real priorities. A company called Goodman, Fielder & Wattie telephoned from Hong Kong to ask us if they could sell Harry Ramsden's fish and chips in a special promotion at Kai-tak Airport. They had the catering concession there and a base of British expatriate customers had been lamenting the absence of good old British fish and chips.

We had no money to support an event like this. We could not let anybody use our name without sacrificing our standards. We asked Cathay Pacific if they would sponsor our flights, which they agreed to do in exchange for photo opportunities to publicize their new Manchester–Hong Kong route. Marketing Judo. We asked our fish supplier to pay for the fish. We approached Holiday Inn to pay for hotel rooms. They all agreed. More Marketing Judo. Finally we asked Goodman Fielder for a fee and they countered with the offer of introductions to interested franchisees. Yet more Marketing Judo.

Despite a battle when we arrived there to get the basics right – including the first ever Harry Ramsden's wok-fried fish and chips – the event was a stunning success. There was a queue of 50 expats throughout the five-day promotion. People were driving two hours across the island to the airport to eat fish and chips! We appeared in full colour on the front page of the *South China Morning Post*. The pictures were wired back to the UK and a massive free PR campaign followed.

We found a franchisee who, two years later, opened a large Harry Ramsden's on the island in Wan Chai in a blaze of publicity. Ten years of big business followed until the lease expired after the handback of Hong Kong to the Chinese Government. The restaurant had a great write-up in the *Rough Guide to Hong Kong*. We got thousands of travellers and tourists on our side as they returned gratefully from Mainland China and a diet of snake and birds' nests to the unexpected refuge of fish, chips, mushy peas and Yorkshire tea in Wan Chai!

Doing the Unexpected. Who would have expected to hear classic arias from La Bohème in a fish and chip shop? Every Monday evening opera professionals sang to a packed audience. They performed twice, before and after Harry's Special – a large portion of fish, chips and mushy peas. the

OPERA & CHIPS

It's not over until the fat lady eats her supper

Fancy Mozart with your mushy peas? Then get down to Harry Ramsden's for a musical feast.

Source: Express Newspapers
Photo: Ross Parry

charge was only £17 for this unique experience! For £100 each we got the stars of the chorus from the local opera company to come and sing for their suppers. Monday night is graveyard night in the restaurant business. But in our places we had six-month waiting lists for customers who would never normally have ever put us on their eating out agendas. So unexpected was it that Radio 2 broadcast one evening live and Calendar ITV and various regional BBC stations broadcast snippets from the event over the years. One opera 'affishionado', as we called them, confided in me that she preferred the Harry's performances to lots of the real four-hour ones! This brilliant idea came from our local franchise partners, George Osztreicher and Joe Parness, in the Cardiff Bay restaurant who conceived it when the Welsh Opera House failed to get funding. They did the unexpected, used their brains rather than a budget, got the crowd on their side and filled a dead Monday night. We exported this idea everywhere and repeated the success of the lowest budget opera production ever. Doing the unexpected means investing when everyone else is downsizing; buying at lower prices in recession when everyone else is sitting on their hands; using lower share prices to buy shares for your Employees Share Ownership Plans; hiring talent when the slothful fat cat companies destroy it by 'downsizing'. Zig when they zag. Do the unexpected. Be the flexible nimble Smallco and throw the bloated fat cat Sloth. That's the charter for Marketing Judo.

Zig when they zag. Do the unexpected.

CHAPTER 7

KEEPING YOUR BALANCE

THE BENEFITS OF PLANNING FOR THE UNEXPECTED

バランスを保つ

baransu wo tamotsu

MJ Expect the unexpected. This is the final move. It's all about keeping your balance, staying on your feet when external pressures try to knock you over or using those forces to make your own winning move. We know all about external shocks, as the big company strategists call them. We are the people who completed the acquisition of La Tasca restaurants just in time at 2 am on 11 September 2001! Twelve hours later, after the World Trade Center attack, nobody was 'doing deals'. We are the people who were in the middle of our float when the Chancellor of the Exchequer resigned and the stock market crashed. We are the people who almost went bust when the bank pulled out on us a year after we had bought the business. Expect the unexpected. The rule today is that the goalposts keep moving, to mix football and judo sporting metaphors. There are no constants. You have to expect and get used to constant change. You have to plan for disaster because it is going to happen. It's just a question of when, not whether. Size makes no difference.

On 14 August 2001, the chairman of the world's largest energy company sent an e-mail to all his staff. 'Our performance has never been stronger', he gushed. 'Our business model has never been more robust. We have the finest organization in American business today.' On 2 December 2001, Enron went bust. It was the biggest collapse of any business in history.

A company that had been chosen as a partner by Enron crumbled with it at breath-taking speed. Years and years of expensive brand building marketing went down the drain as the name Arthur Andersen was shredded by association with Enron.

Whatever your size, you have to keep your balance. You have to make contingency plans. You also have to be ready to tear up all those plans, which took so long to prepare, and switch course. Sit back complacently and you are yesterday's fish and chips. You are as good as the last plate of tapas your team served. Take yourself too seriously, congratulate yourself on how well you are doing, read your own PR once too often, and you will be thrown by that smaller competitor who has just come up with a new move. It's hard to do this as a small business.

Just think how hard it is for the big company competitor to change course. He has much more to lose and can't react nearly so quickly.

The most unlikely things do happen. Other people play Marketing Judo with you and some don't follow the rules. Foul Marketing Judo! A red card. It's called *Hansoku* in Judo. Shortly after we took Harry Ramsden's public, a Jersey-based company wrote to us with an ultimatum. Either pay them £250,000 or they would tell the world that they had registered our trademark in 20 different countries and planned to set up fish and chip restaurants under our name. This would have been really embarrassing, as we had made a lot out of our international ambitions in the float prospectus. Trademark pirates were boarding us: we were in trouble. I then got a call from a lawyer representing the Jersey company. He asked to meet me in a bar in

Covent Garden. 'Are you wired up?' was his first question. This was a long way from business, as I knew it. He explained that the trademark piracy was his scheme; the Jersey company was a front. He then offered me a share in it!

I went round to our lawyer Mark Copping who took down all the details and prepared statements for my signature. We then sought and obtained an injunction restraining the pirate. We had to contest every trademark application they had made in several jurisdictions. We won in the end but it cost us a lot of wasted time, worry and money. Keep your balance. And in case there are any pirates reading this who want to play foul Marketing Judo with us, I can confirm that it is too late. We own the trademark for Marketing Judo and are investors in The Restaurant People Group, which owns the La Tasca trademark!

The key is to keep your balance. If you have a clear vision of where you want to go, you must not let temporary distractions knock you off course. Unexpected things will happen. Paradoxically, you will be able to cope with them better if you expect them.

We had another unexpected meeting with the underworld of business. A former banker who had just left Ford open prison telephoned Richard to ask if John 'Ramsden', who was a fellow inmate, really had the rights to sell the Harry Ramsden's franchise. This man was claiming to be Harry Ramsden's son. The real son Harry Ramsden's Junior had become our 'Ambassador' and fish and chips mentor. We knew the family history well: we were facing a 'con'. The banker told us he had even written a business plan for John 'Ramsden' while inside. Unfortunately he hadn't got an important basic right. John was an impostor who had changed his name by deed poll to John Ramsden. When we told the real son, he revealed that he had received calls from the police because the impostor had impersonated him many times. The false son's speciality was to seduce wealthy older women and persuade them to pay for a Harry Ramsden's franchise – up to £25,000 a time – before he disappeared.

Back in the legal world of Marketing Judo, you have to have alternative plans tested and ready to go for all occasions. The days of long-term predictable plans are past. We laugh when our former colleagues still inhabiting the dinosaur world of Sloth-like big companies tell us about the contortions they go through to write five-year plans. September 11 has reminded everyone that business lives are short. In 1999 dotcom companies were valued at astronomic price–earnings ratios and funds were raised with back-of-the-envelope business plans. One year later most of them were history.

Small companies are much better at keeping their balance in this environment. It's so much easier for us to try some new moves. We don't have the clutter of management hierarchies to convince. We know that it's tomorrow that counts rather than the intellectual masturbation of five-year plans. We know that you have to expect the worst. Most importantly, we know that we have to have an exit route planned for our shareholders. Is this a marketing issue? In our view everything is a marketing issue. Too few companies have marketing at the centre of their companies. Everyone should be a marketeer, whatever their functional role. Everyone can use the Marketing Judo framework.

In 1998, an unexpected event occurred. Share prices in our sector of the market began to fall. Restaurants, once the darlings of the City, were now out of favour. The average price–earnings ratio dropped from 25 to 15.

To cap it all, our venture in Melbourne, Australia, ran into trouble. We fell out with our franchise partners in Harry Ramsden's least favourite country and the business suffered. But we had tested contingency plans in reserve. One of our team, a fellow founder Director, Richard Taylor, had consistently led the way in championing contingency plans. He was the one who kept us on our toes, challenging us to expect the unexpected! He had been the 'champion' of a project to trial smaller kiosk outlets on motorway service areas with Granada PLC, which were working well. Another of his projects, a separate takeaway company under a different name run by a joint venture partner Maurice Gammell, was making big profits. We persuaded Maurice, a brilliant entrepreneur and natural Judo player, to sell his 50% share in the takeaway company and join us as MD. We managed to keep our balance through a very difficult period. We had an exit route available because we had picked the right partner in the successful Granada motorway test!

Granada subsequently approached us about selling to them. We had become an important element in their plans to introduce brands to their business. Our stock market rating was not likely to get back to the heady days of 40 P/E ratios in 1996! It was time to do the unexpected. In November 1999, we agreed to sell.

Of all the unexpected things that happened in the Harry Ramsden's story, the most unexpected to me personally was on a trip to Singapore. This is also one of the Marketing Judo moves that I am very proud of. Now you have to appreciate that I am a frustrated football player. You see, my dad and uncle were very good players. Both played for Wimbledon – a small club which, incidentally, used to be brilliant at Marketing Judo! They won the FA Cup in 1988 with a team that cost a fraction of the losing club Liverpool. My dad won an amateur cup winner's medal in 1937. My uncle played for England as an amateur. I love the game but unfairly the family soccer genes skipped a generation. So you will understand how thrilled I was in Singapore.

We were looking to sign up a franchisee. I arrived at a famous Orchard Road hotel after the 13-hour flight from London, went up to the reception desk and gave my name. I was told to wait while a manager was summoned. He arrived, whisked me away and took me straight up to a magnificent top floor suite, overlooking Orchard Road. Now I was confused. I was jet-lagged. I knew we had used Marketing Judo to get the Leeds travel agents to negotiate a cheap deal. They had probably argued that I was an important future customer from a giant PLC!

The suite was fantastic. There were flowers, champagne, a jacuzzi, walk-in wardrobes. This was an outrageous deal, brilliant Marketing Judo. Then I read the letter from the manager: 'We are proud to welcome you to our hotel. Please accept this with our compliments. We would be grateful if you could come to the Board Room on the second floor at 9.30 am tomorrow. We would like to take a photo of you with our hotel football team.' Guess what?

They thought I was THE John Barnes: the former Liverpool and England football star! Three key differences exist with my namesake. First, he is 20 years younger. Second, he is a good footballer. Third, he is black and I am white. There is absolutely no chance of confusing us.

Marketing Judo believers pick the right partner. They get the crowd on their side. They use their size to their advantage. They do the unexpected. They keep their balance. So I duly went to the boardroom at 9.30 the following morning. The press were there in force. The hotel team were kitted out in their strips. The cameras were poised. Nobody paid me any attention. I approached a player. 'Hello', I said, 'I'm John Barnes.' He stared at me, bemused. 'No you are not John Barnes', he replied in haltering Singaporean English. 'Yes, I am', I continued, 'I am John Barnes from Harry Ramsden's.' He looked shocked. 'But you are not a footballer', he stuttered. 'I am John Barnes, the Chippie', I declared with a large grin. 'Oh No!' he exclaimed.

The press decided it was a wonderful story and pictures were taken. Later I was asked to wear a Liverpool shirt.

CASE OF FISHTAKEN IDENTITY

Hotel thought white chippy was Barnsey

Source: Express Newspapers
Photo: Ross Parry

The picture ran in the largest selling paper the next day. The story was picked up back home. I appeared on page 3 of the *Daily Star* under the headline 'A Case of Fishtaken Identity'.

It was news in every quality paper. The story was even run on the *Mark and Lard* show on BBC Radio 1. This really impressed my kids! We calculated that the press and media exposure for Harry Ramsden's would have cost £250,000!

I had used all the Marketing Judo moves. I had even played Judo with myself. I awarded myself a black belt as I drank the free champagne. . . . Move 7 – *Keep Your Balance!*

CONCLUSION

So there you have it: Marketing Judo. It's not a panacea. We are not trying to claim that every move works every time. We are suggesting a framework you can use, a thought process to help you. Try it. Ask yourself:

1. Where can we improve the basics?
2. Whose assets can we lever? Which partner shall we pick?
3. Which Sloth-like opponent do we choose?
4. What can we do to get more of the crowd on our side?
5. How can we be more agile (the three 'F's)?
6. Which competitor can we unbalance?
7. Who or what might be about to unbalance us?

If you want to do this in more detail go to 'The Marketing Judo Game Plan' (Chapter 9). You can contact us on our website: www.marketingjudo.co.uk.

CHAPTER 8

MARKETING JUDO SENSEI

EXAMPLES OF GREAT MARKETING JUDO

In this section we have selected six companies that have impressed us by using their brains rather than their brawn! All of our examples started their lives as small operations with scarce resources.

To whet your appetite we begin with sandwiches, crisps and beer!

1 Pret A Manger

This company, in a sector that we know well, is inspirational. It is privately owned. They opened their first outlet in 1986 in London and have grown to over 120, with two in New York and new stores opening in Hong Kong and Japan.

In a market characterized by 'greasy spoon' cafés and shops selling tired traditional sandwiches and stewed tea and coffee, Pret broke the mould. They started with the basics, building a kitchen in the basement of their first shop in Victoria, and going to the food markets at dawn every morning. Freshly prepared on site every day, Pret's sandwiches kept the traditional British triangular shape with a choice of fillings including new, healthy alternatives, merchandised in self-service racks.

The brightly lit modern design positioned the new concept well away from conventional sandwich shops. Anticipating the move to US-style coffee shops, Pret adopted fast service coffee equipment and drinks from cappuccino to espresso well before the arrival of Starbucks and others.

Well-trained and motivated staff are visible to customers as they sit in team talks before the stores open. The basics are right.

Pret has the right partners running it. The founders, Julian Metcalfe and Sinclair Beecham, have remained at the helm since the start. Observers have commented on their complementary skills. As they say on their website: 'We are passionate about our food, our staff, and our customers.'

Their brand's consistency and integrity have much to do with Sinclair and Julian's passion for their brand, and their continuity of direction and ownership. They have recognized the need for succession by bringing in a Chief Executive, Andrew Rolfe, with experience of running larger organizations.

Their choice of McDonald's as a 33% investor rather than an IPO fund raising has been controversial but ensured that they remained in control, and leveraged McDonald's property expertise in the USA and international markets. Clever corporate venturing for both companies. They share similar people-focused cultures and values. Pret has partnered a Geesink and avoided a potential competitor.

From an early stage, Pret got the crowd on their side by offering every day all their unsold sandwiches to charity to help feed the homeless. This reinforced their freshness positioning and resulted in brilliant press and customer word-of-mouth support.

In a market notorious for labour turnover, Pret has been selected by *Fortune* magazine as the 9th best company to work for in Europe. They encourage career development and offer appraisals every four months and well-structured training. Their staff are wonderful ambassadors for their company. As one employee was recently quoted as saying in a big regional paper feature: 'They don't tell you to do things, they ask you with a bit of politeness. At the end of the day, the manager always says "thank you".'

They move in terms of product innovation with the agility of good Judo players. New flavours, ingredients, coffee strengths and openness with customers set them apart from most other retailers. They are certainly the 'fittest, fastest and most focused' in the leisure sector.

They have done the unexpected by opening in the USA and the Far East. They repeat 'the little touch that means so much'. The story told on the side of the passion cake box says it all:

"Thirteen years ago Colin Lloyd and Kate Cherkoff appeared at our first shop with a sample of their Passion Cake. Using only 100% natural ingredients, no preservatives or artificial flavours, the taste was out of this world. Last year Colin and Kate travelled to Manhattan to share their secrets with Marc Hayman, our baker in New Jersey, who shares their passion. Marc now produces six varieties of cakes and slices for our shops in New York."

They kept their balance when they wanted both to release some capital and raise more, without risking the whims of the public stock markets, by partnering with McDonald's.

Pret is a brilliant Marketing Judo player.

2 Kettle Foods

This is another company that has spotted a niche in a big volume market – the potato crisp industry – and developed a unique selling proposition. The story of Kettle Chips shows that you can take on the big guys and win.

Cameron Healy founded Kettle Foods in the USA in 1978. He began with no working capital selling cheese and roasted nuts to natural food stores. On the back of this, he developed a new business. He went back to the basics of potato 'chips' or crisps by cooking sliced-by-hand 'real' potatoes naturally straight into the fryer (just as Harry Ramsden did). He pioneered a new segment in the American crisp industry, taking on the giants of the industry, who had steadily reduced the taste and quality of the 'good ole' potato chip by automation, producing hybrid potatoes and using artificial flavours.

In 1987 he met Timothy Meyer – a fellow American – on a trip to the UK and came face to face with the British passion for crisps and a market full of pale imitations of the real thing. They established a company in Norwich to supply Kettle Chips to the UK market. They developed special packaging to protect the quality and flavour of the Kettle Chips.

Picking the right partner has worked for them. First, they picked each other and are still the private owners today. Next, they got going in Norwich by 'partnering' an existing crisp company that had surplus space. They rented an empty part of the factory where they installed their Kettle Chips equipment. After five years of successfully introducing their unique product to the UK market, they moved to a new and larger site in Bowthorpe, Norfolk.

They clearly believe in 'getting the crowd on their side' and 'using their size to their advantage' sharing a passion to maintain a commitment to 'the community, to its people and to the culture of constant quality improvement' as they say on their website. They don't use TV, unlike the big boys in the sector; they rely on word of mouth, PR and strong community involvement through their community liaison officer.

They 'did the unexpected' by calling their product 'Kettle Chips' rather than 'crisps' in the UK market. They 'kept their balance', in the cut-throat crisp market where supermarket own-label products proliferate and where so many small companies have failed. In the process they built a £50 million business.

3 Cobra Beer

This is the smallest of our selected companies. They have 'partnered' Indian restaurants in a unique and imaginative way. None of the Sloth-like British brewers would ever have deigned to target this niche so cleverly. The basic premise of this business is that ordinary beers and lagers don't go well with hot, spicy Indian food. Cobra developed a beer that complements the food really well. Having picked their partner in the large and popular £2.5 billion Indian restaurant market, they have also picked on an ideal opponent in Carlsberg lager.

Cobra developed their recipe with an Indian brewer. The first production was authentically done in India. India versus Denmark (home of Carlsberg) was a contest with an obvious winner 'in front of a crowd' of Indian restaurants. Cobra's larger initial packaging – 660 ml for sharing – further differentiated them from the competition.

After early success, production has moved to the UK where they have picked a good partner in Charles Wells, a leading UK independent brewer. Cobra is now the top-selling premium-bottled beer in the Indian restaurant market.

The founder and owner Karan Bilimoria is a great media advocate for his company. He has achieved tremendous free PR by regularly speaking publicly and getting the media crowd on his side by charmingly telling his small company success story in the business press. The beer has won quality awards, thereby generating more PR.

Cobra beer is now sold in supermarkets, which will further build the brand. This is a small £10 million turnover company built from scratch by using the weight and strength of India to its advantage. The top-selling beer in Indian restaurants, created in the UK and now brewed in the UK, is a true exponent of Marketing Judo.

4 Eddie Stobart

From sandwiches, chips and beer we move to a transport company with a big consumer brand. We have been amazed by Eddie Stobart's appeal ever since a leading PLC's Finance Director confessed to us that he was an Eddie watcher, collecting the names of the trucks as he travelled the motorways. One of our trainers at Harry Ramsden's resigned to move to Australia and marry one of our team she had met there. This was probably the only good thing to emerge from our antipodean misadventure! For her leaving 'do', we planned a surprise visit from an Eddie truck driver and a farewell ride in the lorry. She was one of the 25,000 members of the Eddie Stobart fan club. The Eddie Stobart Company co-operated brilliantly. Unhesitatingly they agreed to send a truck and driver to the Guiseley restaurant. Our trainer bade farewell to Harry's with two circuits of the car park in the cabin of her favourite truck. The driver was a wonderful ambassador for his company.

This extraordinary tale of a trucking company with a cult following, selling high quantities of branded merchandise and a brand image to rival the best fast-moving consumer companies is a shining example of our 'Get the crowd on your side' Marketing Judo move.

The business was founded on great basics. Eddie Stobart – like Harry Ramsden – named his son after himself. The son Edward set up the trucking business in Carlisle in 1976. He began with eight vehicles and set a new standard for this part of the service industry by branding his trucks and drivers with a distinctive colour and uniform design. Each truck has a different woman's name emblazoned on the front, which became the focus of the truck-spotting cult. There is a cartoon character – Steady Eddie – that is winning the next generation of truck spotters.

Behind this marketing spin was a very efficient integrated storage and distribution service. The company grew steadily with depots opened throughout the country. It is Britain's largest independent haulage company with over £150 million turnover.

Eddie Stobart's employees are really proud of their trucks and their company. They have built the reputation of the brand through word of mouth. The trucks and drivers are travelling billboards that advertise the brand, the company and its values without the cost of advertising and promotion.

This is the best example of using brains rather than budgets that we have seen in any industry or category.

5 Channel 4

Channel 4 costs the taxpayer nothing. It has no predictable upfront licence income like the BBC. Unlike the ITV companies, it has no big institutional shareholders to fund it. It cannot draw on the vast resources of the Murdoch Empire, as can the Sky channels. It has to earn its keep from advertising and subscription income. When advertising revenues fall as they did after the September 11 'shock' Channel 4 had to become a corporate 'guerrilla', it has no war chest. It has to use its brains to fight its battles. Channel 4 is a brilliant exponent of Marketing Judo. It is a rare and possibly the only example of a public–private partnership working. By having to work harder than its competitors it creates a better brand. Channel 4 gets the basics right by producing innovative content that grabs the attention of their audience, and then wins new viewers by creating free marketing in every other print or broadcast medium.

Thus *Big Brother,* their pioneering real life soap, is so relevant to its audience that it becomes the main feature discussed in both the top selling tabloid newspaper, owned by Murdoch, and on the number one show on Radio 1, owned by the BBC! They have levered the weight of two far bigger competitors, one a Geesink (Murdoch) and the other a Sloth (BBC) to their own advantage. World class Marketing Judo! We believe that Channel 4 succeeds because it has to connect better with its audience to survive. Big budgets can destroy creativity and fuel bureaucracy. The Sloth's lair becomes populated with consultants and 'Lovies'. Channel 4 in contrast partners underpriviliged minorities and so uses emotional leverage to grow its fan club. Whether it is investing in broadcasting the Kumbh Mela religious festival, or putting thousands of school kids in estates through summmer cricket school, you know that their fatcat competitors would never do it. And that is how you build a brand. Not by sticking to the ordinary, but by unbalancing your competition. By Doing The Unexpected (Move 6).

Channel 4 never stops innovating. In the latest series of *Big Brother* they are levering the fascination of their audience with voting on who should be evicted from the house, to generate income. Links have been created via betting and gaming to bookmakers!

Where ITV failed to master Digital television and threw in the towel, Channel 4 with tiny resources have fought on with E4. In the harsh climate of 2002, they 'took a fall' and closed FilmFour Production's business. New top management continued to run rings round the ITV companies by being fitter, faster and more focused.

Originally Channel 4 went head-to-head with Sky to acquire the rights to broadcast UK horseracing and tap the huge betting revenues available. Astutely aware they might lose the bout with the Geesink, they nimbly opted for a winning move by partnering successfully with Sky in the 'attheraces' joint venture.

Their coverage of cricket has broken the mould by harnessing new replay and computerized camera techniques to enliven the action. For the 2002 India versus England test matches,

Channel 4 have partnered a number of Indian community projects and another Sensei – Cobra Beer – to play Black Belt Marketing Judo.

Channel 4 are brilliant marketers because they have to be. Brains beat budgets. If you need inspiration tune into Channel 4!

6 The Geesink Example: Walkers

And finally, we have chosen one superstar big company with whom we would never like to compete. Geesink showed that size *did* matter when he beat all the smaller guys at Judo through combining skill and size. He forced a change in the rules and the introduction of weight classifications. There is one company in the UK crisp market who have all the characteristics of the best small company but are owned by Pepsico, one of the world's largest corporations.

Walkers Crisps began life as a small Leicester company. Pepsi bought them in the 1970s. Resisting the temptation to globalize the brand and use their successful international Frito-Lay name, Pepsi picked the Walkers brand as their UK partner. They have preserved the Leicester origins, picking a celebrity who famously played soccer for Leicester FC, to get the crowd on their side. He is one of the British public's favourite personalities – Gary Lineker. The Walkers Crisp TV ads are so good that people talk about them. The company has even built Gary's name into the branding with 'Salt-and-Lineker' flavoured promotional packs. This is a celebrity who won't bring your brand into disrepute. He is brilliantly managed by his agent, Jon Holmes. We met both Gary and Jon in our time at Harry Ramsden's and concluded that we would never want to play on a team against either of them.

Walkers are constantly innovating with new flavours, pack designs and TV ads. They have also made their first move into the premium adult snack market with the launch of their 'Posh' crisps – Sensations – linking Victoria Beckham with

Gary Lineker. Their 'occupation' of highly expensive floor space throughout the largest superstores in the country reflects a highly skilled and motivated sales force.

This is a Goliath of the international marketing world that convinces the public that it is a local, truly British company. Walkers and Geesink would be an equal match for each other if they swapped trades!

CHAPTER 9

THE MARKETING JUDO GAME PLAN

Finally, we often get asked: 'How can I put Marketing Judo into practice?' Well, one way is to put together a Marketing Judo Game Plan for your business.

We use this idea in our Marketing Judo Workshops, where we take each move and ask a series of questions to help participants create their own Game Plan. On the following pages we have selected the questions that we most frequently ask and which apply to most businesses. As you go through them we hope that they will trigger other questions that are specific to your own circumstances.

1 Getting the basics right

The first three questions are fundamental to your business but need to be addressed before you start to play Marketing Judo.

→ What are the key basics for your business?

→ What evidence do you have that you really have got them right?

→ What action must you take to get them right and how long will it take/cost?

Once you have satisfied yourself that you have the core basics right, then you can move on to the next set of questions which form the first part of the Game Plan itself.

Key brand proposition

→ What makes your business different/stand out from your competitors?

A good way to help you understand what makes your business different is for you and your team to describe the 'Brand Personality' for your own business and for your key competitors.

You can do this by imagining the different businesses as people and describing their key characteristics. For example: Are they male or female? How old are they? What do they wear? What kind of car do they drive? Where do they shop? The questions are endless and really bring the business to life for everyone.

It's amazing how creative your team can be in painting the pictures and how helpful it is in creating a clear personality for your company. It's even more fun to do the brand personality exercise for your competitors. Do the exercise for each competitor so everyone can have a copy.

The exercise can also help you define what you would like to be in the future and what changes need to be made to your business if it is to reflect the personality you would like it to become. It can also be a lot of fun as well!

Another good test is to take your own and your competitors' literature, cover up the company name, and see if you can tell whose it is. It's amazing how hard it sometimes is to tell them apart. If one company's proposition does stand out and you know immediately who they are, then the odds are they are a very successful business.

Key support

→ What justification do you have for making this claim?

It's no good having a very clear and different proposition if you can't back it up. It is unlikely that your customers will find it credible and their trust in you will be diminished. It will simply be 'guff'! (The Yorkshire for 'spin'.)

Key target audiences

→ Who are your primary and secondary target audiences for your business?

Unfortunately, you can't talk to everyone and you have to make some hard choices here.

→ Does what makes you different/stand out from your competition have real relevance to them?

This is the time to revisit your key proposition and make sure that it is relevant to your primary target audience. If it isn't, then think again.

You may like to write down your answers and then ask each of your team to do the exercise without telling them what you think. Then compare notes. Their answers may be very revealing and give you the opportunity to discuss the differences. Getting consensus from the team could be a key action step here.

MARKETING JUDO GAME PLAN

ACTION:	NEXT STEPS	TIMING	RESPONSIBILITY

2 Picking the right partner

In this move you are looking to identify whom you can lever, who is going to be a *willing* partner and who will be prepared to co-operate with you. Some helpful questions here:

→ Whom are you already partnering and what more can you get from the existing relationship?

→ Who else can you identify to work with to help you build your business?

→ What can they add that you can't do for yourselves?

→ What are the benefits of picking them as a partner?

→ What are the risks – if any?

→ Who will benefit most from the partnership?

→ What are the benefits for them to partner with you?

→ What principles drive their business – are they broadly the same as yours?

→ In what ways can you make sure that you will get more than 50% of the benefit for less than 50% of the risk/cost?

→ Whom have your competitors successfully partnered and can you persuade them to partner you instead?

The purpose here is to identify all the possible partners for you to play Judo with. Remember: the more powerful the partner, the greater the opportunity for you to apply leverage and therefore derive benefit. However, good Judo is 'win–win' and your partner should derive some benefits too, otherwise the relationship is unlikely to last very long.

MARKETING JUDO GAME PLAN

PICKING THE RIGHT PARTNER

ACTION:	NEXT STEPS	TIMING	RESPONSIBILITY

3 Choosing the right opponent

Unlike the previous section, where you are looking to partner for mutual benefit, here you are looking for an opponent to compete with and overcome.

You need to understand your opponents' strengths and weaknesses so that you can clearly identify whether they are 'Sloths' or 'Geesinks'. Some questions you might ask are:

→ Which of your competitors are 'Sloths'?

These are the ones you love to take on. They are usually slow to react to changes in the market. They are arrogant and complacent. Their customers often complain about them and the poor service they provide. They may think of themselves as 'Geesinks' but that is only an example of their arrogance.

→ Which competitors do you like to be up against the most and which the least when pitching for a contract or customer and why?

This question will help you to select the Sloths to compete with rather than the 'Geesinks'. It will also help you to assess the strengths and weaknesses of your opponents and to focus on how you can defeat them.

→ What is it like to be a customer of your competitors?

It is often possible to try this out as a private individual. The odds are that the treatment you receive will be typical of what most customers receive. Spot the opportunities for your business.

→ What do your customers think of your competitors?

It is often surprising what they will tell you. It may not be the same as you think from your perspective. Once you have identified their weaknesses, then you can use your Judo skills to exploit the opportunity.

→ Which competitors are part of a multi-division organization?

These are often very large organizations that have been weakened by their lack of focus. The division you compete with may have resources taken away to shore up some other division within the group, which makes them an easy target.

→ Why not try a 'brains day not budget day?'

This is an excellent way to encourage your team to outwit the competition. You ask them for all their ideas to help you market your business, which don't require a marketing budget to execute.

The key here is to get them to choose the best ideas by asking them to rank them on a scale of 1 to 10 with 1 being the least popular and 10 being an absolute winner. Those that get a 10 will get done because there is a commitment from the team. For those ideas that score lower, say 7, ask the team what would need to be improved or changed in order for them to give it a 10. Any ideas that don't at least make an 8 are unlikely to work because the commitment has not been given.

However if an individual in the team really believes in an idea and personally gives it a 10 then let them go ahead – some people love to prove themselves right – and you wrong!

MARKETING JUDO GAME PLAN

CHOOSING THE RIGHT OPPONENT

ACTION:

NEXT STEPS	TIMING	RESPONSIBILITY

4 Getting the crowd on your side

This is the emotional leverage move. Some questions to ask here are:

➜ Who is the crowd in your business?

The crowd can be made up of a number of different groups, depending on the business you are in. However, most businesses have customers, staff, consumer or specialist media, local communities that are important to them where they may have factories, offices, distribution centres, etc.

➜ What more can you do to get them on your side?

Think of each of these groups individually and come up with a plan that addresses each of them and shows how your company makes a positive difference to them.

➜ What initiatives are you taking that could be of interest to either local, national or specialist trade press?

As we say in the chapter, it is amazing what you can generate from what you are already doing but may not have communicated to the outside world. Think of these first and then move on to possible new initiatives.

➜ How can you make yourselves more available to the media so that you become the first one they think of when they want a quote?

This move takes time but often your bigger competitors will avoid the media rather than court them. You will make your company look much bigger than you actually are if you are prepared to put yourselves forward. Perhaps you can create an event that the media will want to cover.

→ Which of your team could benefit from a media-coaching course?

Most people are nervous of making a mistake when talking to the media. By putting your key people through a media-training course (including yourself), a large part of those concerns can be removed or substantially reduced.

→ When was the last time that you asked your staff or customers for their views?

Everyone wants to be valued and the simplest way is to ask them what they think. If your culture is right, then they won't be afraid to tell you. The more involvement and ownership they have, the more you will get them on your side.

(See next page for Game Plan.)

MARKETING JUDO GAME PLAN

GETTING THE CROWD ON YOUR SIDE

ACTION:	NEXT STEPS	TIMING	RESPONSIBILITY

5 Using your size to your advantage

This is all about the 3 'F's – Fit, Fast and Focused. If you are small then these should be your strengths.

➜ What are the training programmes for all your staff?

Fitness in Marketing Judo is all about training. You and your staff cannot rely upon brute force. By being better trained and fitter, you can defeat larger opponents. If you have scarce resources, then you may be able to get help from government-backed initiatives that are available (the ideal Judo partner!).

➜ What are the ways that you already move faster than your competitors and how could you do even better?

Speed of decision making must be quicker if you are smaller. If it isn't, then you are at a real disadvantage. One of the dangers that fast-growing companies face is the ability to take decisions quickly if they all have to be taken by one person. If this sounds familiar then review your process fast –before you become a small 'Sloth'!

➜ What stops you focusing on the key issues in your business?

Focus is one of the key strengths of the expert Judo player. This is the ability not to be distracted by the unnecessary nor to fall in love with the latest new idea at the expense of the core business. By all means explore new ideas, but if you try to follow too many paths at once then you'll get lost.

➜ In what ways can you keep all your staff informed with regard to your objectives and how you are all performing?

One of the key advantages to being small should be your ability to communicate with your staff and make them feel that they are a part of something special. Large organizations really struggle with this and often end up with platitudes at best and company songs at worst! 'Think big – act small' is a good way to tackle this one.

MARKETING JUDO GAME PLAN

USING YOUR SIZE TO YOUR ADVANTAGE

ACTION:	NEXT STEPS	TIMING	RESPONSIBILITY

6 Doing the unexpected

Doing the unexpected gets you noticed and helps to change how people think about you. Your Game Plan will be stronger if you can come up with some initiatives under this heading. It applies not just to your opponents but also to your customers and staff.

→ What would be 'doing the unexpected' in your business?

Maybe there are things that people have said: 'That can't be done in this business.' Why not? If there are really good reasons then fair enough, but if it is simply because they haven't been tried out before, then you may be able to steal a march on your competition by being the first to do it.

→ What would be unexpected in your business that your customers would really like?

Often it is the little things that get remembered that are a pleasant surprise. They may not cost very much but it is the thought that counts and gets you noticed.

→ What move would put your competitors off balance and allow you to gain the initiative and how do you keep them off balance?

Once you have your opponents off balance, it can help you to use some other moves to keep them that way. Don't just think of the first unbalancing move but ask yourself what the follow-up moves might be to keep them off balance and eventually defeat them.

MARKETING JUDO GAME PLAN

DOING THE UNEXPECTED

ACTION: NEXT STEPS	TIMING	RESPONSIBILITY

7 Keeping your balance

This is the only defensive move – but a critical one if you don't want to end up flat on your back!

➜ Who or what might unbalance you or cause you to take a fall?

This is a good one for you and your team to brainstorm. Most of us do our best not to let negative thoughts get in the way of running a business, but in this move let your imagination run riot! After all, it is better that you think of it before it actually happens or before your competitor does!

Having thought of all the doomsday scenarios, then the group must also come up with the solutions. If you can't think of a solution then appoint someone to be the champion to develop one – fast!

➜ What happens in a crisis?

Hopefully your brainstorming session has identified the likely cause of a crisis. But what happens when the crisis strikes? Do you know who to contact and how to contact them? Do you have a crisis management team? Who will speak to the media? Who will talk to staff, customers and shareholders?

If you don't know the answers to these questions, then you will have difficulty keeping your balance.

➜ What legislation could cause you to lose your balance?

The burden of legislation is increasing all the time and smaller businesses often find it difficult to keep pace with the changes. What are the hot issues for your business and how are you dealing with them?

→ What are the trends taking place in your market and are you prepared for the future challenges?

Sometimes you can be so focused on making your own moves that you fail to see what could be looming towards you. The changes might be quite subtle in some cases but suddenly you realize that you have become stranded. What could these be for your business?

(See next page for Game Plan.)

MARKETING JUDO GAME PLAN

KEEPING YOUR BALANCE

ACTION:	NEXT STEPS	TIMING	RESPONSIBILITY

Recommended reading

David Yoffie and Mary Kwak's *Judo Strategy* (Harvard Business School Press 2001), who published their book while we were writing ours! (We had registered the name 'Marketing Judo' as a trademark in March 2001 and had given our first presentation on Marketing Judo in 1996.) Their book is a 'must read' for those who would like to take the Judo analogy even further into their overall business strategy and read about some examples from the US.

George Thompson's *Verbal Judo* (William Morrow 1993). He is a former American policeman who also found that Judo principles worked for him. Subsequently, thanks to his innovative approach, thousands of other American policemen benefited from his example.

Enjoyed this book?

We hope so. And we'd love to hear from you – what you thought of it, your experiences of marketing judo and your views on the individuals and companies that are contenders for best players in business today.

You can email your comments direct to the authors:

john@marketingjudo.co.uk
richard@marketingjudo.co.uk

and/or to the publishing team via **www.business-minds.com** (click on the feedback button).

So, whether you'd like to share a real-life anecdote of your own, or whether you'd like to tell us what you think and what you'd like to read more about, just drop us a line. We'd be delighted to hear from you.

John Barnes, Richard Richardson
and Prentice Hall Business

MARKETING JUDO WORKSHOPS

Build your business using Brains not Budget

Join John Barnes and Richard Richardson in one of their workshops and practise applying the Marketing Judo moves to your business.

The workshops are run for groups of individuals from different businesses or in-company for specific teams.

They have worked successfully for Directors, Partners and Managers in small, medium and large-sized businesses.

Using a combination of presentation, discussion and feedback techniques, the workshops help you create a Marketing Judo Game Plan for your business. They are entertaining, with real life stories, anecdotes and practical tips on how to use your brains to market your business when funds are short.

If you want to join us on the Marketing Judo mat for a workshop, visit our website at **www.marketingjudo.co.uk** or contact us at our e-mail addresses:

john@marketingjudo.co.uk
richard@marketingjudo.co.uk

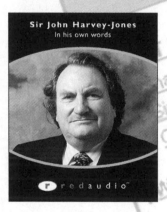

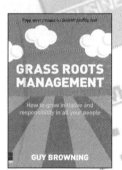